OÙ EST LE

CW00428709

OÙ EST LE 'PING'?

GASCONY – THE FULFILMENT OF A DREAM

GRACE McKEE

ILLUSTRATED BY THE AUTHOR

An imprint of
**ANNE LOADER
PUBLICATIONS**

This book is dedicated to my dearest husband Phillip, without whom there would be no fulfilment of dreams, to my beloved children, Stephen, Kathryn and Sharon who do not realise what they have been missing and, of course, to our many friends in Gascony who prove that warmth and caring transcend all language barriers
Grace McKee

ISBN
1 901253 11 2

Published November 1999

© Grace McKee

The moral right of Grace McKee to be identified as the author of this work has been asserted by her in accordance with the Copyright, Designs and Patents Act 1988.

All rights reserved. No part of this publication may be reproduced, stored in a retrieval system, or transmitted in any form or by any means, electronic, mechanical, photocopying, recording or otherwise, without the prior permission of the copyright owner.

Published by:
Léonie Press
an imprint of Anne Loader Publications
13 Vale Road, Hartford
Northwich
Cheshire CW8 1PL
Gt Britain
Tel: 01606 75660 Fax: 01606 77609
e-mail: anne@aloaderpubs.u-net.com
website: http://www.aloaderpubs.u-net.com

Designed and printed by:
Anne Loader Publications
Covers printed by Delamere Graphics, Hartford

Grace with her husband Phillip

About the author

Grace McKee is a pathologist who can quite accurately be described as suffering from chronic wanderlust. She was born in India and lived in at least ten different towns and cities, qualified as a physician and then left to train in New York for a year. She next moved to England where she married and produced what she considers are her three best achievements – her children.

She trained in pathology at St Thomas's Hospital, London and then was head of the department of Cytopathology at the Royal Surrey County Hospital in Guildford for 12 years. Her husband Phillip is also a pathologist, and a well-known author of medical textbooks. Having decided 'if you can't beat them, join them', Grace wrote a medical textbook of her own in 1996.

During her years in England she travelled widely, from Europe to Israel and the Far East, Japan, South Africa and the United States, mostly to conferences, combining them with short holidays.

Grace and Phillip moved to Boston, USA, in June 1998. She now works as a pathologist at the Massachusetts General Hospital and is Assistant Professor at Harvard Medical School.

Grace's many extracurricular interests include sewing, embroidery, crochet, needlepoint, watercolour and oil painting, and also drawing. She has done her own illustrations for the book.

List of illustrations

Contents

Larroque – a haven of peace in glorious Gascony

Chapter One

A bit of trickery

Although it is almost seven years since we bought our ancient stone farmhouse in France I still feel the occasional, very fleeting, twinge of guilt about the way in which I tricked my unsuspecting husband Phillip into viewing French property. However, I know he doesn't hold it against me, in fact, I'm often praised for my part in finding us a haven of peace in our otherwise incredibly busy working lives.

Even now the evocative fragrance of lavender takes me straight back to France no matter where I am. France to us has always been a heady mixture of fragrant flowers and herbs, warm, sleep-inducing sunshine, stunning chateaux and, of course, tasty, satisfying food.

Our passionate affair with France started many years ago when we lived in England, with short trips to Paris to see the sights and experience the wonders of this magnificent city. Strolling along the banks of the Seine, having my portrait drawn (rather inaccurately) by a pavement artist in front of Notre Dame, licking our fingers after a delicious sugar and *marron*-filled *crêpe* or two, marvelling at the symmetry and beauty of Versailles only whetted our appetite to see more of this intriguing country.

Short detours on the drive back to the ferry port confirmed this overwhelming desire and I began to subscribe to several French magazines which showed us the beautiful sights that were yet to be seen. In addition, there were pictures of charming, though often tumbledown, barns and farmhouses also elegant chateaux in need of restoration at ridiculously low prices, all of which were begging for renovation. My all-consuming desire to own and do up one of these properties was not shared by my more pragmatic husband who pointed out that we could not afford a second mortgage no matter how appealing the property. Even my pleas for a home in a warm, sunny area of France that would be perfect when we were old and ridden with arthritis fell on deaf ears. However, persistence is one of my strong points and I spent hours poring over figures to show that we could buy a small property in La Belle France and still eat. Nevertheless he was stubborn and I had to bide my time.

Fate was on my side. Phillip, my husband (or 'significant other', which seems to be the preferred term in the United States where we now live) was offered the use of an apartment on the shores of Lake Annecy for a week in return for some training he had done and left me to plan our trip.

Not a minute was wasted. I spent hours reading the various books I had bought on France to decide which area would suit us from the point of view of climate and scenery. I certainly did not want to purchase a property in an area where the climate was similar to that of England and the attractions of the micro-climate of the Charente were strong. Yet the descriptions of Provence in Marcel Pagnol's books were irresistible as were the awe-inspiring mountains of Languedoc-Roussillon. The Dordogne was out of the question because there were too many English people living there and we had often spoken of living a French lifestyle among French people. I eventually ruled out Provence because of the high cost of its properties and the alarming incidence of burglaries of holiday homes. One of our friends has had his property in Clermont-Ferrand burgled so many times that he now leaves the shutters wide open so that potential burglars can see that there is nothing of value inside.

Telephone calls to various estate agents in England who were involved in selling French properties yielded much more information from very helpful people, most of whom had second homes themselves in France. I was told that the Vendée was rather flat and had quite a penetrating farmyard smell, that homes by rivers often required higher insurance because of the danger of floods and, yes, Provence was prohibitively expensive unless we wanted just an apartment. There were the additional problems of the mistral and the cold winters there. The climate in Normandy and Brittany was similar to that of Surrey so unlikely to be of interest to people who wanted long hot summers with little likelihood of frost in winter.

With the help of a kind estate agent in Portsmouth who was a Francophile herself, we planned an itinerary starting with an overnight stay in La Chataigneraie, visiting two or three properties in several *départements* such as the Vendée, Charente-Maritime, the Gers or Gascogne (Gascony) and Languedoc-Roussillon. From there we would drive to Lake Annecy and spend two or three days in our friend's apartment.

June 20, 1992 dawned clear and bright. I had been up till 1am chatting with my younger daughter Sharon but leapt out of bed at 3.30am when the alarm rang. We left for Dover at 4.15am and were the first car at the ferry terminal. We were both excited about the trip to France and I was finding it extremely difficult to keep my secret about viewing properties. Phillip drove off the ferry and meekly followed directions as I was the official navigator – a role that accepted the responsibility for any mistakes made by either the map-reader or the driver, even if the latter ignored the navigator's instructions. We started off on the smaller, scenic roads but soon realised we would have to take advantage of the *autoroutes*, the wonderfully maintained French motorways which were the shortest distance between major cities and towns. I had never driven on the 'wrong' side of the road before so was quite content in the passenger seat. However, when while driving along the *périphérique*, the ring road around Paris, Phillip started dozing, the fear of a crash far outweighed the concern about driving on the right, especially as we had stopped in a precarious position on the hard shoulder. I took the wheel and gingerly pulled out, my unhappiness made even worse by the fact that it was pouring with rain and the Parisians drove as though escaping from disaster with no patience for a timid woman driving a car with British number plates at a snail's pace. I had no choice but to keep up with the rest at 80 miles per hour, fervently praying that our guardian angels were working overtime. After a refreshing nap Phillip took over the driving and we thundered on to La Chataigneraie.

We finally arrived at our *chambres d'hôte* around 9.30pm and were shown to our room which had enough space in it for a smallish double bed and a little bedside table. A sliding door in one wall exposed the diminutive bathroom with shower, wash-basin and toilet. This was France and we loved it.

We were directed through a small alleyway to the dining room which was warm and buzzing with excited, chattering, gesticulating French families. A little Yorkshire terrier who seemed to be part of the establishment danced for food and was certainly well rewarded. Phillip's steak and my omelette with *champignons* (mushrooms) laced with garlic tasted every bit as good as the aromas promised. Replete, we retired to bed for our first encounter with the hard, sausage-like bolster lying where the pillows should have been. Some time during the night we surrendered, slid the bolster onto the floor and used our folded jackets as pillows.

The next morning after a quick shower we indulged in a *petit déjeuner* (breakfast) of warm, fresh *croissants* and *baguettes* with butter and homemade *confiture* with more chunks of fruit and more runny than the jam we were used to in England.

The hotel staff and the other guests were friendly and curious but we could not understand most of what they said. Eventually we said '*Au revoir*' to our new friends, mistaking their '*bonne journée*' for a good journey rather than a good day! Phillip had studied French in school many years before so was familiar with French grammar but his vocabulary was not so hot. My French vocabulary consisted of two words '*oui*' and '*non*' at the inception of this project. However, with the help of the BBC and Berlitz French on the Move tapes which I used to listen to religiously driving to and from work, I had picked up a lot of useful conversational French and increased the number of French words that I could recognise to a remarkable extent. Although I did not anticipate asking for directions to the Café Flore, the basic question certainly stood me in good stead whenever we were lost. Whether I understood the answers fired back at me is another matter!

8am: Seated in the car, map on lap, ready to leave – definitely time to confess. Surprisingly, Phillip took it well, seeing the funny side of it and made me promise not to buy any property unless it cost almost nothing and definitely not until we had long discussions first. He also mentioned that what we could afford would buy a lopsided, roofless barn and not much else, but there was no harm in looking. I felt much happier and started to enjoy the trip having unburdened my soul to my beloved husband.

We drove through peaceful villages with clean, tree-lined streets, neat stone houses with pots of brilliant pink and purple petunias guarding the front doors and spilling out of window boxes. In the distance we saw magnificent chateaux with inviting *dégustation* signs but we had no time to stop for wine-tasting, we had important business to attend to involving appointments with several estate agents. It poured with rain again but that did not diminish our excitement one little bit.

Our first estate agent was an English lady who had moved to France with her little daughter for personal reasons. She had not lived there very long and was extremely nervous about driving or, for that matter, finding the two properties we were to view so Phillip drove and I navigated. The first house we saw was typically Charentais, a small farmhouse with a tiny kitchen and a bedroom built on a platform projecting into the barn where the animals used to be housed. In days gone by the family and animals lived together, the heat from the barn rising to warm the bedroom. The small plot of land that was being sold with the house was a couple of fields away and could only be reached by climbing a stone wall and braving the animals in an adjacent field. This was not for us. We had envisioned a small house but one large enough that family and friends could stay with us for holidays, preferably in separate rooms.

The next house we saw was quite appealing. Part of it had been the village *café tabac* and there was a huge square room in the front with the original chairs and tables stacked along one wall. The house was in very good condition. Next to the large room was a small kitchen, which could only be entered from the little courtyard and then a small bathroom which again only communicated with the courtyard. A staircase in the kitchen led to the two small dark bedrooms upstairs. On the other side of the courtyard was a row of buildings for the animals. The house had grapevines growing along the walls and there was a half-acre garden at the end of the courtyard. When we were asking directions to the house, the farmer's wife who helped us insisted on getting into the car to direct us and did not stop talking all the while we were there. She came into every room with us and asked the estate agent more questions than we did. Next she started interrogating us, with very little luck as she spoke so fast that we could not understand her. We did like the house but it cost more than the measly sum we had tentatively agreed on so we decided to move on. However, we were not allowed to leave until we had driven the farmer's wife back to her home to meet her husband, a tall, meek man who did not speak much. He did not need to.

Our new friend who had not seen any English people for a while reluctantly said goodbye and we then drove on to Baignes where another expatriate British estate agent showed us some more properties. One of the more memorable ones was a huge townhouse with a massive garage and adjacent solid teak front door opening directly onto the street. The hall was wood panelled with a carved wooden staircase connecting four floors. There were bedrooms and bathrooms on each floor and in the kitchen downstairs was a smaller staircase which led to another cluster of bedrooms and a bathroom, originally used by the servants. The one-acre garden at the back was a haven of peace with no indication that it was in the centre of a village. The old lady who owned the house was seriously ill in hospital and the house was being sold to pay the hospital bills. Although the price was embarrassingly cheap, the thought of cleaning fourteen bedrooms while arthritic and of a pensionable age was not appealing and we decided to keep going. Even the gentle threat of a builder from Nottingham who was interested in the property and would be buying it that evening if we did not decide immediately did not affect our decision. We hoped it would be sold quickly to pay the old lady's bills and were sad at the thought of her having to leave the house she had lived in and loved for seventy years.

Our next stop was at an *immobilière* (estate agent) in Montréal du Gers, a beautiful village perched on a hill bursting with flower-filled pots on lamp-posts, on patios (*les terrasses*) and in window boxes. The trees lining the streets were growing in precise, straight lines with impatiens creating a riot of colour around their bases. The village square or *place* had a profusion of bright flowers growing in every available space and the ancient stone of the surrounding buildings glowed warmly in the summer sun. What a lovely place to work in, we thought, comparing the view with the dirty grey buildings we saw from our workplaces back home.

Again, we were fortunate to have an English estate agent, her colleague being a handsome green-eyed Frenchman who spoke English with a charming accent, much more pleasing to the ear than our feeble attempts at French.

We saw three houses, all of which were interesting but not quite what we were looking for. One was a little house perched on top of a hill with just two rooms and a bathroom. The views were magnificent but the location seemed to be miles from anywhere. How would we get our daily *baguette* when we were too old and infirm to drive? The next house was a cute little square one, converted from an old farmhouse to look like a doll's house. Inside there was a new pine staircase and pine furniture and the whole appearance was unreal, apart from the house being too small even for the two of us. Our long-suffering estate agent Jean took us to another property. It had been renovated using part of a large, old farmhouse and was still part of it. We had to tramp over a field to reach the front door and the alterations were not yet complete. The front door led straight into the living room/kitchen, which had a beautiful wooden staircase and galleried landing leading to the only bedroom and a tiny bathroom. It was being sold by a Parisian couple who had started the renovations but ran out of money. We did not think we could help them out, especially in view of the rather steep asking price.

Jean then drove us back to Montréal du Gers and directed us to a nearby restaurant for lunch while she conferred with the green-eyed Henri.

Chapter Two

Où est la salle de bains?

*H*enri collected us from the restaurant, gesticulating frantically for us to hurry as there was a property that had just come on the market, indeed he did not have all the details as yet, but would like us to view it.

He drove very fast down the narrow roads, often driving in the middle of the road and turning right around to emphasize a point and check our reactions. The surrounding gently rolling landscape was tranquillity itself with perfectly straight rows of deep green grapevines interspersed with fields of paler green young sunflower plants. Distant clumps of trees sheltered old farmhouses, the more affluent ones with their status symbols — *pigeonniers,* round or square towers which in times past housed pigeons, valued for the fertiliser they produced. On either side of the winding road there was a deep ditch and the tendency for French drivers to tear down the middle of the road irrespective of what might be around the corner was a bit nerve-racking, especially as our thoroughly charming driver drove in the same manner. Fortunately we did not collide with any oncoming cars, nor did we land in a ditch but tore down a lane and screeched to a halt in front of a small single-room barn with an outbuilding behind it. The roof was missing and there was nothing else to view. This was not suitable accommodation for cows, never mind people! Even Henri was perplexed and drove us to the house of the farmer who was selling the property. Apparently we had gone to the wrong place, the house for sale was down the next lane.

The farmer, his wife and two children, a girl aged fifteen and

Our first view of Larroque with the stable on the left and a dead tree stump guarding the property.

a boy of sixteen, accompanied us to the house which was five minutes' drive away. At the end of the lane we stopped in a clearing in front of a large, ancient stone house with climbing roses on either side of the front door and grapevines draped along the side wall. Attached to the left of the house was a huge barn and attached to the barn and built on to it at right angles was a stable, obviously newer than the rest of the house. On the other side of the clearing, facing the house was a large open barn filled with circular bales of hay. At the side of the stable was a pond or *étang* filled with bulrushes. The side of the house and the front of the stable faced south and the view in that direction was of rolling hills with farmhouses and reservoirs dotted at intervals amongst the textured fields. Behind the house, separating it from the main road was a gentle hill

11

G. McKee

Rotten shutters, broken windowpanes and cobwebs greeted us when we first saw Larroque, but they only added to its charm.

that was wooded. Half the wood and the fields surrounding the house, an area of two and a half acres, were included in the sale. Facing south, at the edge of the clearing there were overgrown rose bushes bearing heavily scented blowsy roses, canna plants, box and laurel, all inter-twined with infiltrating thorny blackberry stems. Underfoot the crushed mint plants gave off a refreshing fragrance. Beyond these, on the downward slope of the hill grew lilacs and more laurel. Peering through these I saw another level area below the main house with a smaller building which was the chicken house. This seemed to be in better condition than the main house, with a large run.

There was another large but dilapidated brick and timber building behind the open barn facing the main house and yet another outbuilding behind the stable in which stood some ancient farming equipment, so rusty that to move it would result in its disintegration to reddish brown powder. Growing beside this outbuilding was a large fig tree with tiny green figs hiding behind the large leaves. The field beyond the open barn was somewhat overgrown and in the centre was a small well next to which was a fig tree covered with brambles.

The roof of the house appeared to be in a fairly stable condition and had the tiles and scalloped edging typical of the region. The front of the house was covered with dirty grey rendering which had chipped off in areas revealing the beautiful golden stone underneath, identical to that forming the side wall. The old green wooden front door did not quite reach the doorsill, the two front windows on either side of the door were of different sizes and had rotting green shutters. The floor above had a large square shuttered opening, which was originally used to load grain onto carts. There were several small openings in the walls at the level of the first floor – these were to air the *grenier* or attic where the grain was stored. The south-facing wall was covered with a profusion of sweetly scented old-fashioned roses intermingled with grapevines. The walls were stained with bluish green patches which, we later learned, were due to the copper sulphate used to spray the grapevines. The barn had huge zinc doors which were misshapen and did not reach the ground. The stable had a rotting stable door and a smaller shuttered window above.

We were invited inside and stepped into a hall with a floor of cracked but attractive tiles which were alternately yellow and crimson. The first room on the right was small and had a fireplace and parquet floor which had seen better days. The wallpaper was a bright orange with large flowers and was peeling off in strips. Cobwebs covered the windows. The second room off the hall was larger with half-panelled walls and a wood ceiling, both of which showed overwhelming evidence of woodworm. The hall ended in a shelved cupboard again full of cobwebs and packets of rusty nails. On the right was another door leading to a huge kitchen with a fireplace six feet across,

The old-fashioned rose and grapevine growing along the south-facing wall. The roots of the vine grew up between the tiles of the kitchen floor.

the walls of which were blackened through decades of use. A thick iron chain with a hook at the end hung down over the grate; this was traditionally used to hang the cooking pot in which the day's meal simmered over the fire. There was a window in the south-facing wall with a view over the roses and the chicken house. A small stone sink, with a single tap and cold running water, was directly under the window. Another ancient, cobwebby cupboard filled with old tins, packets of nails and jars of fat stood in a recess on the right of the window. The floor was covered with the same yellow and crimson tiles we noticed in the hall, but again most of them were cracked. The outer kitchen wall seemed to sag and there was a long iron bar that ran from the front to the back of the house through the kitchen. We were told that many French houses had this type of supporting rod holding the walls together as they did not have proper foundations. On the left of the hall cupboard was a door which led to another room. It was dark and eerie and on entering it we stepped unexpectedly onto soil. A rotting stair-case led to the attic and behind it, up a couple of steps was another door which led to yet another room. This one had peel-ing wallpaper as well, a tiled floor and a bread oven. The wood ceiling, the walls, doors and the bread oven doors were stud-ded with large rusty nails, presumably on which things were hung. A single window with rotted shutters and broken glass illuminated the room. Working our way back through the kitchen, we found another door leading to yet another room. This backed onto the room with the bread oven but did not communicate with it. It was a dark, scary room with a single window facing south and a wooden partition along one wall. One half of this was the sleeping area furnished with an old wooden bed covered with piles of musty bedding. The other half was a space containing large clay jars filled with fat, prob-ably animal fat that was saved to prepare *confit* of duck and goose. We were told that this was the bedroom of the old lady (the grandmother of the farmer's wife) who lived alone in the house after her children married and had died nine years before. The house had been unoccupied since then. This bed-room also had a fireplace that backed onto the one in the large kitchen but it had a large dark wooden mantelpiece practically hiding it, again covered with the ubiquitous rusty nails. An old wooden cupboard leaned to one side in the centre of the floor.

We gingerly climbed the rickety stairs to the *grenier* and found ourselves in a large airy attic, again filled with cobwebs, dust and the inevitable rusty nails. Huge wooden beams

The side and back of Larroque, where the animals used to live.

supported the roof and the view through the ventilation openings in the south-facing wall was spectacular. However, we still could not see the Pyrenees which were only an hour's drive away although Henri said there were times when this was possible. The wooden floor was more or less intact except for a couple of areas above the kitchen and front room where the holes in the floor enabled us to peer into the rooms below. An old rusted iron and wood weighing machine sat on the floor with a thick iron chain beside it. This was probably used to weigh the grain before it was poured through the large opening over the front of the house into the carts waiting in the clearing below.

We then walked around the house to the back and saw a number of small rooms and hutches built into the wall of the main house, where the animals lived. The wall that was continuous with the back wall of the barn contained a door which led into a small room overlooking the interior of the barn. This contained a circular wooden contraption that was used to crush grapes. The juice then flowed down channels into three large wooden vats in the barn. The previous owners made their own wine many years ago it seems. Emerging from this upstairs room we noticed yet another door in the back wall, this part being the back of the stable. We entered to find ourselves in a large room in good condition, forming the upper floor of the stable with a large window at the front and a trap door to the stable below. The floor was littered with dried corncobs – food for the four-legged helpers on the farm?

We then strolled around the pond at the side of the stable and found ourselves back in the clearing at the front of the house. In front of the pond was a large square washbasin with a tap and running water. Henri told us that the clothes were washed here many years ago. Now the ubiquitous brambles were crisscrossing the washbasin, half burying it. We still had to investigate the stable. The floor and walls were in very good condition, better than those in the main house and there was stabling for three horses. There were also three mangers and, hanging on one wall were two stiff, dusty braided rings which we were told were made from the spermatic cord of oxen and were greatly sought after by collectors. There were also two ancient farm carts at the back. The condition of the stable with its room above immediately brought to mind an independent annexe for guests with a sitting room and small kitchen on the ground floor and bedroom above. A bathroom could be built within the barn which we were about to enter. The covered, enclosed barn was about thirty feet by twenty feet with stone walls, a roof continuous with that of the house and stable, but no floor, just earth. The walls were covered with thick nails from which hung a variety of iron rings, chains and hooks. A door at the back led to the wall that had the built-on animal quarters.

The enormous open barn that faced the front of the house had a tiled roof and wooden walls along three sides, all of which had gaping holes that let in sunlight and trailing stems of ivy. It was filled with circular bales of hay and was exactly the right size for conversion to a four car garage. On one side of it grew a large pear tree and behind it were blackberry bushes and neatly piled logs of wood.

Having viewed the property at some length one glaring problem became obvious. There was running water and electricity, but where was the bathroom? In fact, where was the toilet? There were no signs of either and we were too embarrassed to ask the farmer or his wife. We did not speak good enough French anyway, and it did not seem fair to ask the young daughter although she spoke English after a fashion, having studied it in school. Nevertheless, when Phillip and I were told the asking price for the property we felt it was too good a bargain to miss. We stepped aside to confer and in two minutes

The open barn facing the house, where our friend Pierre stores his hay. The roofs of his home are just visible in the distance on the left of the picture.

decided this was the spot where we wanted to spend our retirement. We knew that the summers were very hot, the winters were cold but frost was unusual more than one day a year. The farms around us grew sunflowers and grapes, most of which were destined to end up as the renowned Armagnac and, of course, the famous *melons du Gers*. There were surrounding orchards of peaches and plums, the latter achieving fame as *pruneaux d'Agen*.

The house needed a lot of work, the most pressing of all being a bathroom and W.C. but we had several years ahead of us before we would even think of retirement and what better time to renovate a house than when one is still working?

I could picture lying in a hammock in the shade during our summer vacation while Phillip mowed the lawn that he would have laid. When suitably refreshed I would tend the garden that I would have carefully planted, a miniature Monet's garden in Gers rather than in Giverny. We would have open fires in the winter and would renovate the stable for guests. I could just picture the barn as a covered courtyard with exotic plants, perhaps even pawpaw and mango, never mind minor details such as the climate being unsuitable for tropical fruit.

In the meantime Phillip's imagination saw the covered barn as a huge music room with a gallery on the first floor adjacent to the grape-pressing room, huge speakers and lots of comfy seats for any neighbours who cared to listen to Berlioz or Philip Glass at full blast.

I could see clearly where the arcade of grapevines would be planted, to provide shade for all those alfresco meals. I knew where I wanted terraces placed so that I could wander down to the chicken house to collect eggs, picking some fresh herbs on the way back. We would have our own grapevines and press our own grapes, perhaps even trying our hand at a semblance of Armagnac. Phillip would be in charge of all the planting and pruning of the vines while I could be relied upon to taste the grapes when they were ripe. Of course, I would bake all our bread in the bread oven, and perhaps a goat might make a good pet as well as providing *fromage du chèvre.* Who could tell, our woods might even harbour secret truffles as well as the oaks and sloe bushes that were visible! Perhaps we could even add prestige to the house by building a *pigeonnier* (with old stone, of course).

Well, that was it! We talked ourselves into making an offer for the house, Larroque, and were rushed off to the *immobilière* to telephone the estate agent in Roussillon and cancel all other appointments.

Jean and Henri took us to a beautiful, elegant hotel in the nearest big town, about 15 kilometres away. The hotel was built of the beautiful golden stone of the region with an impressive stone staircase and beautifully decorated and furnished rooms. The antique *armoires* and solid, comfortable furniture were enhanced by the well-chosen drapes. The proprietors Sylvie and Armand are a lovely couple who have become good friends of ours over the years. They seemed as delighted as we were that we were buying a property nearby and very generously opened a bottle of high quality Armagnac to celebrate the occasion. Sylvie and Armand are both excellent cooks, Armand usually dealing with lunch which was served in the small restaurant they also owned adjacent to the hotel and Sylvie providing the evening meal for the hotel guests.

We could barely sleep for excitement that night. What a bold pair we were, buying a second house when we still had a mortgage on our home in Guildford and had four children still being educated! On the other hand, we now had a holiday home as well as a place we could happily retire to and a very good reason for visiting France as often as possible. We did feel remorse at not getting as far as the apartment near Lake Annecy and never got a reply to our letter of abject apology. In fact, we have never heard from the owners since.

Chapter Three

Down to brass tacks

*T*he next morning dawned fair and clear although we probably would not have noticed had it poured with rain. We had a delicious *petit déjeuner* with proper coffee, freshly squeezed orange juice, soft buttery *croissants*, small bread rolls which were crisp and crumbly on the outside and soft inside, slices of home-baked bread with nuts and fruit, butter and three types of Sylvie's home-made jam — *confiture aux fraise, pamplemousse ou melon.* Needless to say it took a while with the help of gestures and drawings on the paper napkins for us to understand that the first two were strawberry and grapefruit. I instantly resolved to ask Sylvie for her recipe once we owned Larroque and could harvest our figs. Phillip's response was to just finish all the jam on the table to show his appreciation. The lovely fresh rolls were perfect for dunking in one's coffee as the French do.

I now know, several years later, that I made a horrendous mistake that first morning. The *croissants* looked so flaky and buttery that I let Phillip have mine and it became a family tradition that he would have both our *croissants* whenever we were in France. Somehow he did not care for the British version. It was only much later that I realised what I was missing when I ventured to try a small piece, but had to face much opposition when I suggested that perhaps it was time he let me eat my own *croissant*. We now have to order three so that I can enjoy one.

Jean appeared on the dot of nine to take us to *Monsieur le Notaire* in Lectoure, another well-known town about 15 kilometres away from the little village where Larroque was situated. We drove along roads lined by trees on either side, providing dappled shade, with fields and gently rolling hills in the distance. Lectoure is an enchanting town built on a hill, again with beautiful stone buildings, walled gardens and numerous little *cafés* and *bar-tabacs* where even stamps could be purchased. Many of the houses had front doors which opened directly onto the street. The opened shutters on the windows revealed the pretty lace curtains that provided privacy. Some of the more affluent homes had walled gardens and the tops of banana plants and cascading stems of the trumpet vine (*Campsis radicans*) with its bright orange flowers hinted at hidden delights. The *Notaire's* office was airy and welcoming, filled with potted plants. The gentleman himself professed not to speak English and we, of course, could not speak legal French so had to

A typical tree-lined avenue in the Gers.

depend on Jean translating word for word what each of us said. Everything was tapped into his computer of which he was obviously very proud. It was interesting that my maiden name seemed to be very important, although I had been married for years, and all the resulting documents bore Phillip's name and my maiden name.

After a tasty lunch of *soupe du jour* (soup of the day) and sausage with *frites* (chips to us Brits) at a nearby restaurant we returned to the office of the *Notaire* where M and Mme Boivin were already waiting, to go through more formalities. They were homely, honest people who spoke not a word of English, and, what was worse, spoke French very rapidly with an Occitan accent that was totally incomprehensible. The property we were purchasing, Larroque, was 250 years old and had belonged to Mme Boivin's grandmother who lived in it until she passed away nine years before. The money from the sale was to be divided between Mme Boivin and her brother's widow, from what we could understand. According to French law the children also have equal shares in the equity but it was all too complicated for us simple folk to follow. We were still stunned by the magnitude of our folly although this was tempered by excitement.

We left Lectoure somewhat shell-shocked as the harsh reality of what we had done dawned on us. We had put down a deposit on a 250-year old farmhouse with no foundations (but it did have three foot thick stone walls and running water), which needed an awful lot of renovation, we would have to find a French builder to put in a bathroom before we could spend even one night there, we did not speak fluent French so would have to learn it and we would have to re-organise our finances to take into consideration a second mortgage and money for renovation. On the other hand we loved France and had a perfectly good reason for spending more time there now and had many years left before retirement in which we could gradually make the house habitable. As to the lack of foundations, if the house had stood for 250 years it would surely last another 50!

We went back to Larroque for another look and discovered another fig tree beside one of the outbuildings, a pear tree at the side of the open barn, with several others bordering the drive, behind the sloe bushes. Rose bushes bearing a profusion of blooms grew under every electricity post. The brilliant blue of the sky and the warm golden sunshine convinced us that we had made the right decision. Pierre and Marie Boivin from whom we were buying the house showed us around again with young Dominique translating into schoolgirl English – 100% better than Phillip's schoolboy French and my practically non-existent French! This kind family whose home was about five minutes' drive away and whose land bordered on what would soon be ours, was warm and friendly and we have grown even closer with the years. Pierre farmed the land with the help of his son François, Marie ran the house, did all the accounts, reared chickens and quail in season from day-old chicks, grew and bottled vegetables in abundance and potted meat when the pig was ready to be converted to food. More of that later. Dominique was still at school, a very pretty and bright young girl who helped her mother around the house and even drove her father's tractor.

After yet another visit to the *Notaire* the next day we opened an account at Crédit Agricole in preparation for paying the electricity and water bills later. Having said farewell to the Boivins and to Jean and Henri we drove back to the ferry bypassing Roussillon (why look there when we had already seen something we both wanted?). We knew there would still be a lot of paperwork, arranging the French mortgage and sorting out money transfers and so on before Larroque would be ours. The first thing I did on returning home was to buy several Teach Yourself French books and tapes and a good dictionary (Larousse). I even commandeered the children's O level French books in an effort to get to grips with the language.

Most of our friends were congratulatory and perhaps a bit envious, while several immediately said they were definitely going to visit in France. The odd one or two bearers of gloom and doom told us how foolish we were to buy a dilapidated property in a foreign country where people were liable to cheat strangers, what guarantee did we have that the legal system in Lectoure actually worked and had we not heard of all the ex-pat Brits who had to give up their homes in Spain because the government decided that the purchase was not legal? All this did not alarm us in the least; we had considered all these potential problems and had talked in great length to others who had bought property in France (two of my colleagues and three of Phillip's had holiday homes in various parts of the country) and we were not changing our minds.

In the meantime there was a lot of work to be done. Our original English estate agents provided us with details of a firm specialising in arranging French mortgages and we were able to get one sorted out with *Société Générale* in Angoulême. Our English bank manager did not seem terribly upset when we confessed what we had done and all we could then do was wait to hear from the *Notaire* as to whether the transaction would go ahead.

By the beginning of October we started to panic as we had not heard any news from France and Jean could not provide us with any more information. The date was soon approaching when our deposit would be returned to us with a hefty penalty fee paid by the Boivins as it seemed the hold-up was on their side. We knew they could not afford this and agreed to forfeit the penalty payment in return for having the house cleaned before the sale was completed (there was a lot of clearing-up to be done as the house had been unoccupied for years and the old furniture appeared woodworm-ridden, besides I wanted the old lady's bed and bedding removed before we took the house over). Apparently the delay was due to a court hearing to decide how the equity should be divided between Marie and her brother's widow who lived amicably next to each other.

We took the overnight ferry once more on November 11th from Portsmouth to Cherbourg. This route became so familiar to us over the years and although it was always a rush to finish work in time to tear down the A3 to Portsmouth, the holiday mood hit us as soon as we started packing the car. Once on board the ferry it became our habit to dump our overnight bag in the cabin and scoot to the restaurant for a lovely meal, then a quick browse around the Duty-free shop and to bed to be gently (or violently, on certain occasions) rocked to sleep in our bunk beds. The night crossing always seemed to be too short and the rude awakening just before arrival invariably came as a shock. The long drive bypassing Rennes, Nantes, Bordeaux and Agen became a challenge each time as we tried to find the quickest yet most scenic route. The rest and refreshment stops were infrequent as we tried to reach Larroque before sunset.

This first time we wandered off the *autoroute*. The journey took an incredibly long time much to our dismay and we did not arrive at our favourite hotel until 10pm. Sylvie and Armand had left us a message to say they had to go out and they were sorry they could not provide dinner but the owner of the Pizzeria a few hundred yards away was expecting us for a meal. We strolled out of the hotel through the courtyard, crossed the little street and walked up a narrow *rue* between high stone walls with closed wooden shutters and heavy doors. The aroma of oregano and other fresh herbs led us straight to the Pizzeria. We stepped through the large doors into a cosy, welcoming room packed with large chattering families including children of all ages as well as young, lovelorn couples so engrossed in gazing at each other that they seemed unaware of what they were eating. The stone walls were covered in original oil paintings which were for sale. Near the door was a pizza oven which looked like a modern, immaculate version of the bread oven in Larroque with its domed roof. A young man was rolling out pizza dough at great speed, scattering the toppings over the dough and then sliding the pizza into the blazing oven on a large flat piece of wood. The owner, a charming man with dark eyes and a beard, welcomed us as though we were royalty and escorted us to a table in the corner. He seemed to know all his customers and stopped at each table to chat. We warmed to him and his family instantly – the female relatives waited on the tables and were as gracious as the owner. Pizza is one of my favourite foods and I ordered with relish although it was difficult to decide which toppings to choose, as long as artichokes were one of them. Phillip had his inevitable steak and we shared a delicious tomato and onion salad. The dressing which was very simple, consisting of olive oil and lemon, salt and pepper was quickly mopped up with pieces of fresh French bread – when in Rome, do as the Romans do! *Monsieur le Patron* was soon back to converse with us. We haltingly explained that we were there for the weekend to finalise the purchase of our farmhouse, whereupon he disappeared and returned with two glasses of deep red *floc*, a specialty of the region, usually drunk as an *apéritif.* This sweet, almost sherry-like drink rapidly became my favourite when in Gascony, both the red and white varieties. It seems unheard of anywhere else in France.

The next day we drove to our little village on our own for the first time, Michelin map at the ready, passing through a small village with a few immaculately maintained stone houses bordering the road, a petrol station and a small sign in front of one of the houses advertising locally produced Armagnac for sale. At the entrance to the village alternate green- and red-leafed trees lined the road (these had been vigorously pollarded by this time but had been in their full glory in June). There were several humps or 'sleeping policemen' along the road to slow down the tourists who raced through in summer. At this time of year there were no signs of life in the village apart from one old lady in black who was peering through her window at the foreign car driving through. Fortunately for us the petrol station was open and we were able to fill up with *l'essence* although we had to check with our trusted dictionary that we were using the right thing as *gazole* seemed to sound more like gas, the American equivalent of petrol. The lady who manned the pump was friendly and interested in why we were in Gascony off-season. She seemed genuinely delighted that we were buying a property in the neighbourhood and said that it was good thing people were buying and renovating old properties in the region as many were being neglected and ended up as heaps of stones. The younger generation preferred to work and live in modern apartments in the cities rather than toil in the fields. She also said that rich families from Paris and Bordeaux were buying second homes in the region but many of them preferred homes by the sea or by rivers, preferably already renovated, or even newly-built houses. We saw several new houses that were being built along our route but these seemed uninspiring and had none of the charm of the old farmhouses and barns which had been renovated in the traditional style.

We met Jean and the Boivins at Larroque and wandered through the rooms once again feeling a surge of excitement that this was going to be ours very soon. After another visit to the *Notaire* and several more signatures we returned to our hotel and celebrated with one of Sylvie's gourmet meals of delicately flavoured *consommé* garnished with a wafer-thin slice of *foie gras* followed by chicken with red peppers and capers. Needless to say, although we were feeling quite full we just had to try the dessert – *îles flottantes* ('floating islands'). An early night was essential not only because we were replete and could not stay awake, but also we had to leave at the crack of dawn to get to Cherbourg without breaking all speed limits. We arrived in plenty of time to visit the huge supermarkets with their wide range of food, clothing and household goods. We stocked up on a selection of cheeses, wines and olives of varying sizes and colours to take back to family and friends.

December 22, 1992 was a day of great rejoicing as *Monsieur Le Notaire* telephoned us at home to say Larroque was now ours. He spoke very slowly in impeccable English so must have either been practising for months or just did not want to conduct the original transaction in English when acting for both the vendors and the purchasers. The children were delighted to hear that we were taking them out for dinner to celebrate but were a bit crestfallen to find we were going to a French restaurant near Guildford rather than to McDonald's. At the end of the day the French restaurant was a great disappointment – the flavours did not seem quite right and I still have not recovered from having my avocado pear cooked until it was unrecognisable. Nevertheless I cheered myself up by writing one of my innumerable lists, this time of the work that needed to be done to Larroque in order of priority. The mortgage that had been arranged for us included a loan for essential repairs and renovation to make the house habitable, the interest on this portion being miniscule. The arrangement was that we would get the work done by French workmen and send the invoices to the bank for payment from the amount of the loan. If the money was not used by a certain date the interest on it would increase rapidly. We were never ones to drag our feet and the next day I telephoned Jean to enquire about a reliable *maçon* (builder).

Our concern, now that we were French property owners, was that Larroque would be broken into and squatters would take possession having realised that we were away for long periods of time. Our friends with a second home in Clermont-Ferrand had told us an interesting story. When they bought their property they filled it with lovely antique furniture, some pieces being family heirlooms. The first time they were burgled they got all their possessions back by a happy coincidence. Apparently the local *gendarme* was having a quiet cup of coffee at a pavement café when he noticed a large van with the number plates of a different *département* – for example in our area the vehicle registration plates include the number 32. Being a curious sort (or just a really good policeman), he followed the van and discovered a large warehouse filled with stolen goods. Our friends, on reporting the burglary, were taken to the warehouse and able to reclaim their stolen furniture. However, the next few times they were burgled, there was no sharp policeman watching the local traffic, there was no trace of the thieves or their possessions, so the house is now left practically bare when they are in England.

Chapter Four

Où est le ping?

Faxes flew back and forth between France and England with *devis* (estimates) for the new bathroom. Unfortunately this could not be built until the pipes had been laid, a septic tank (*fosse septique*) had been installed and flooring and walls put in where we wanted the bathroom – in the earth-floored room that had the rotting staircase leading to the attic. The hot water pipes had to wait until a boiler was installed, the boiler could not be brought in until the electricity meter was changed to accommodate the increased voltage, and the electricity company (EDF – *Electricité de France*) could not install a new meter until we had become customers. The bathroom suite had to be chosen by us and we had to decide whether we wanted the bidet in the bathroom or in the W.C., and whether we wanted a bath and/or shower.

All these decisions necessitated another trip to France. Fortunately there was a scientific convention that I had to attend in Paris at the beginning of February, a good excuse for a return trip to Larroque. We decided to try the Southampton-Cherbourg route and drove first to Paris. We stayed in our favourite (small and expensive, but conveniently located) hotel and, as soon as the conference was over left for Gascony.

We stopped at the Boivins just to let them know we were there in case they saw lights on in the house and became concerned but were immediately coerced into staying for dinner that night. The Boivins' farmhouse was about the same size as Larroque but in much better condition. There were several outbuildings, one of which housed the washing machine and drier, one the bathroom and another an indoor barbecue. Two or three rusted cars lay abandoned at the edge of the yard and in a penned-off area three large dogs – hunting dogs, we later learned – watched us newcomers with interest. An assortment of chickens and roosters roamed around freely, some perched on rods in the open barn which housed large farm machinery. From the edge of the yard we could just see the outbuildings of Larroque separated from the Boivins' home by large neat fields. We were invited in and stepped straight into the kitchen which was the heart and soul of the house with its roaring log fire in the corner fireplace. The kitchen units, sink, cooker and dishwasher were arranged along the wall opposite the door. Near the large refrigerator was a tall wooden bin containing five or six very large long loaves of bread. In the centre of the room was a long dining table with an assortment of chairs around it. Several of these had cats asleep on them, one kitten was curled up in front of the fireplace and about five small dogs with some terrier-like features but varying coats (some smooth, some curly and some stiff and bristly) gambolled under the table and chairs.

The Boivins are the most hospitable and gracious couple we have ever met. This pressing invitation to eat with them was repeated every single time we visited Larroque and there were always other people there, sometimes neighbours, sometimes Marie's mother who lived in the next house with her daughter-in-law who was Marie's widowed sister-in-law and her three children. She looked after the children while their mother worked. On other occasions there were visiting cousins, aunts or uncles and almost always there was Jules who worked in the fields with Pierre. He was a stocky, sunburnt, jovial man who professed not to know any English but would occasionally interrupt with a 'thank you' or 'goodbye' during our frequent pauses while struggling to find the correct French word. Marie was and still is a wonderful cook. That first meal was memorable. The table was set with a pretty flowered tablecloth and cloth napkins. There were two huge platters of artistically arranged *entrées* consisting of slices of two types of spiced sausage and halved hard-boiled eggs. The egg yolks were a bright golden yellow, not the pale yellow we had been used to. Accompanying this was a large bowl of neatly sliced tomatoes and onions drizzled with sunflower oil extracted from their own sunflower crop and lemon juice, with chunks of home-grown garlic. Plastic bottles of red wine lurched drunkenly on the table. As a matter of interest we have never seen white wine offered or drunk at the Boivins' home. On the modern electric cooker a huge pot of green beans bubbled away merrily and Dominique was busy frying thick potato chips in a deep-fat fryer. In the meantime Marie was smearing mustard onto chickens which had been cut open along the breastbone and flattened with a mallet, ready to grill on the open fire.

"*Entrez, entrez!*" we were told and directed towards the chairs. Both Phillip and I were trying to avoid having any wine as we knew we would not be allowed just one glass and he had to drive back along unlit narrow roads while I had to direct him and needed my wits about me. However, I lost out as I was not driving and, my hesitation being interpreted as a dislike of wine (Marie not caring for it herself), I was poured a fairly large glass of *pastis* to which was added a dash of water. This became my drink and it was poured as soon as I entered their home ever after that first night. It was many years before I plucked up enough courage to be able to say in halting French that I did not really like the stuff.

We had helped ourselves to the delicacies on the table when suddenly there was a loud bellow from Pierre at the head of the table: "*Où est le ping?*"

Phillip and I were totally bewildered, I quickly looked up the dictionary but was unable to find this word and then noticed that Dominique had run across to the bread bin and grabbed one of the very large long loaves of *pain de campagne* (country bread) which she gave to her father. So that was the *'ping'*! We apologised for our lack of comprehension and for the fact that our Larousse had not given us the correct Gers pronunciation of the word. Marie, who is very astute and knows more English than she lets on, explained that this strange pronunciation was derived from the Occitan language or *langue d'Oc*. Words such as *lapin* (rabbit) became *'laping'* and *demain* (tomorrow) became *'deming'*. We were then taken aback to see Pierre holding the loaf of bread with one end against his chest, slicing off large chunks with dexterity. Practice had obviously made perfect – we did not need to bring out our first aid kit.

The meal was delicious! Even the simple *salade de tomates* was so tasty that not a drop of the homemade dressing remained on our plates – we mopped up every little bit with bits of bread like the French did. I was not at all sure what one did with the wrapping around the slices of dried sausage and was relieved to see that everyone else was unwrapping it and leaving the shreds on their plates. The grilled chicken was tender and tasty and, as usual, we both ate far too much. Cheese constituted the next course, delicious Camembert, Brie and a goat's cheese, accompanied by more *'ping'*. Dessert was a huge *tarte* filled with French custard and covered with layers of delicate frilly pastry, much like the filo pastry available in English supermarkets. The Armagnac in the tart lent it added richness. The box of chocolates we had brought as a present paled into insignificance beside this magnificent meal. We staggered out to the car satiated, vowing never to eat so much again, having promised to return for lunch the next day. It was a relief to find our way back to the hotel without getting lost.

The next morning we were up bright and early ready to inspect Larroque where we were to meet Henri who was taking us to Auch, the city of the Three Musketeers, to buy bathroom fittings. Larroque was still standing in spite of the lack of a foundation and the inside was fairly clean. All the old, dark, woodworm-ridden furniture had been removed (though many months later we found the mattress thrown by the side of the open barn). I began the renovation by pulling off the strips of wallpaper that were hanging down in the front room. Unfortunately we did not have any tools handy so I could not attack the rendering that was covering the pale stones of the front of the house. My little notebook was soon filled with lists of items we needed to buy back home and bring with us on our next trip such as pliers, gardening tools, brooms, a dustpan and brush, bucket and mop, floor and glass cleaner, sackfuls of Brillo, gallons of white paint and brushes, dusters and old rags, to start with. We would have to buy the larger items such as ladders and lawnmowers in France. I was also lusting after a mailbox of the type that sits on a post instead of the little rusted metal pocket attached to the front door. This was exposed to the elements and I could just picture our bills and letters gradually changing to papier mâché during our absences.

Henri drove down the overgrown ruts that served as the drive to collect us and then tore along the narrow roads to Auch ignoring all speed limits and driving down the middle of the road as was his habit. We carefully chose the bathroom fittings, all white, deciding that we would have a shower instead of a bath as that would conserve water when our throngs of visitors came to stay. We had decided on a separate bathroom and W.C. each with a washbasin, then Henri reminded us we had to have a bidet, it would be unheard of not to have one installed. I felt the best place for it would be in the W.C. but Henri was horrified at the thought and insisted that it should be in the bathroom. I gave in quietly as Phillip did not have any strong views on the matter. We chose aqua coloured tiles for the walls and floors, again Henri decided that the walls should be tiled up to a distance of two feet from the ceiling, vetoing my suggestion of tiling all the way up to the top of the wall. The shower cabinet was white and was just large enough to turn around in. The store accepted a deposit and agreed to keep the items until our builder collected them. Back at Larroque we drew diagrams of the layout of the bathroom and W.C. on the back of an envelope for Henri to give to the builder (whom we had never met). We then said our *au revoirs* and made our way down the little lane to Pierre and Marie's home.

This time Marie's cousin Anna and her husband Jacques were part of the family gathering. They lived in Agen and often came to spend a weekend in the country. They were a delightful couple who spoke only French but were happy to wait while we stumbled our way through intricate sentences, picking out words from the dictionary with absolutely no idea of what tense to use. They then rattled back in French at great speed, in spite of our plea to slow down, *"Parlez lentement, s'il vous plait"*. Finally Phillip turned to Anna and said *"Madame, vous êtes comme le T.G.V"*. (*train à grand vitesse*, the extremely fast French train) – a nickname that we still often use. Lunch was another culinary delight. We had Marie's special chicken soup with oodles of noodles followed by a delicious coarse *paté* containing small tasty pieces of meat. On enquiring what it was called we were told it was *pâté de tête* which is exactly what it is – a *pâté* made from the head of the pig. Somehow I did not enjoy it as much after being given this bit of information. The main course was a large, fat coiled sausage smeared with mustard and grilled on a rack over the open fire, accompanied by sautéed potatoes and beans that Marie had preserved the autumn before. We had brought a large gateau purchased from the *patisserie* near our hotel that morning but it was not a patch on Marie's cooking. Coffee was produced and poured into little glasses, the box of sugar cubes was passed around but no milk was in sight as the family drank their coffee black and sweet. Dominique dipped her sugar cubes in the coffee and licked them rather than have them dissolve in the coffee. We left the happy group reluctantly: we wanted a little drive around the countryside to learn a bit more about our new home. The kind-hearted Marie insisted on our taking back to England a dozen of her hen eggs well wrapped in newspaper as I had praised the bright yellow yolks of French eggs the night before.

May was an eventful month for Phillip as he had to part with his appendix after a few days of severe abdominal pain. Two weeks later we were back on the ferry to France, this time en route to St Malo. Unfortunately no cabins were available even though we had booked the trip weeks before and we had to make do with reclining seats. These were not too uncomfortable for me but the constant rustling of plastic bags while passengers ferreted around for essential items in the middle of the night ensured that I stayed awake. Poor Phillip just could not get comfortable as he was still experiencing post-operative soreness and he spent much of the night pacing up and down. The drive from St Malo was considerably shorter than our usual Cherbourg race and we arrived at Larroque around 4 pm. To our delight we now had a brand new, beautiful bathroom and toilet (fortunately we had remembered to bring toilet paper!) which were a marked contrast to the dust and decay of the rest of the house. Our kind friends, the Boivins, had lit a fire in the kitchen to warm the house (the thick stone walls kept the house cool) and we remembered that there was a stack of firewood behind the open barn. Phillip was dispatched to bring some more in with strict instructions not to strain any vulnerable areas while I swept the front room and kitchen several times, washed the floors and scrubbed the rickety table that had been lying in the stable. This was at just the right height for our small gas camping stove although two of the legs were precariously balanced on wads of cardboard. I cooked bacon and eggs in the one frying pan we had brought and used the saucepan to boil water for coffee. Our first meal in our new home was good fun even though we had to balance plates on our laps while trying not to overturn the folding garden chairs. Washing up was not particularly enjoyable as we had to heat several lots of water in the small saucepan.

I had this urgent desire to empty and rigorously clean up the jars of fat that we had transferred to the stable until I could do something with them. I first had to scrape out all the fat and dump it in plastic bags, then I boiled water in our saucepan to clean the jars. When I was satisfied that they were clean and dry they were allowed back in the house, in the various fireplaces and, filled with bulrushes from our pond, added a lovely touch to the bare rooms.

Not having a trailer we had brought only the bare essentials for a camping weekend but this did include an inflatable mattress. Pumping up the mattress was a long and laborious procedure as the tubing attached to the bellows slipped out of the mattress connection with monotonous regularity. Pierre had had the foresight to leave us light bulbs and an old gas heater which quickly warmed up the bedroom. However, when Phillip tried to lower himself on to the mattress on the floor the discomfort in his abdomen was so great that we eventually decided to cut our losses and drive to our comfortable hotel. We were lucky to get the last vacant room and sank into the comfortable bed heaving a sigh of relief. Larroque certainly needed a lot more in the way of creature comforts! On hearing of our plight Sylvie and Armand offered to order us a bed and have it delivered to Larroque during our next visit. We gratefully accepted. Our weekend flew past in a flurry of washing floors. It became my routine from that visit on to wash all the tiled floors practically as soon as we entered Larroque so that we could put our cases down without them becoming incredibly dusty. The strange part was that no matter how often I washed the floors the water would still be a dusty brown and the floors never got really clean. The dust of years was not prepared to yield to a foreign broom and mop. Part of my ritual was to wash the floors before we left in the vain hope that they would stay clean until our next visit.

Before our departure for leafy Surrey the Boivins drove across to see the new posh bathroom accompanied by another visitor, a middle-aged, very talkative lady who wore a neat, flower-print dress, apron and slippers. The slippers were a bit of a puzzle but we later discovered that many older French women in our area were inseparable from their comfortable slippers except when they went shopping. We were introduced to her as *"les anglais"* as the Boivins seemed reluctant to address us by our first names. This was our other neighbour, Janet, who owned much of the land that lay south of our little patch. We could see Janet's pristine home with its well-tended garden beyond the reservoir (which she also owned) and felt slightly ashamed of our abundant weeds and brambles. We had thought Anna was the speaking equivalent of the T.G.V. , but Janet's speech was nothing less than machine gun fire. I looked at her helplessly while Phillip smiled charmingly and shamelessly retreated to find some long-lost article in the house, probably a rusty nail! Janet's accent was even stronger than Pierre's and Marie had to translate for us. It appeared Janet was pleased we had bought the property and were renovating it as it would have otherwise joined the increasing numbers of derelict homes which eventually became piles of stones. I told her in my best Berlitz French-tape accents the sexes and ages of our children, and what we did for a living (not in too much detail because saying Phillip cut up dead people – he is a pathologist, not kinky – was difficult enough without trying to explain that I was one too but only examined cells under a microscope).

Before we left for England we toyed with the idea of moving one of our large carts out of the stable to try to establish where it should go when we were finally living in Larroque. It would look beautiful cleaned up and filled with a brilliant array of flowering plants. On second thoughts it seemed like too much effort as we would only have to cart (!) it back in again. We also had visions of auctioning off the bulls' spermatic cord head rings, possibly taking them to the Antiques Road Show first in the hope that they would be worth several thousand dollars but this did not seem likely. They are still gathering dust but in a safe place in case we suddenly get lucky.

Chapter Five

Summer à Larroque

In July 1993 Phillip had to fly to Glasgow for a weekend meeting, a perfect excuse for me to return to Larroque and do some more cleaning and gardening. My friend and colleague Kay, who is also a Francophile and owns property in France, agreed to accompany me for the weekend. She came well prepared with a folding camp-cot, secateurs, a small saw, garden shears, canned food and sandwiches for the long drive. She even remembered tea towels.

We packed my little car with all the essentials and anything else I could cram in including gloss paint and brushes for our new bathroom doors and off we went. Kay was now the navigator with the Michelin map and my list of the major towns and cities in the order that we passed through or around them. This became another obsession of mine. Every time we drove to France I had to note the time of disembarking in France, the roads taken, the distance in miles between towns, the time at which we reached them and the cost of the tolls. I am convinced this will become vital information in years to come.

We stopped at a picnic spot en route for lunch, climbing onto the benches which were attached to the picnic table and unpacked our feast of sandwiches, hard-boiled eggs, tomatoes and fruit. We did have paper towels to serve as napkins but certainly felt like peasants when a French family occupied the table next to ours. The children were sent off to play, the grandfather and father went to *les toilettes*, the mother wiped the table then spread a spotless tablecloth and laid out napkins, proper plates, glasses and cutlery, ably supervised by the grandmother. We could detect no trace of the *'ping'* pronunciation so we knew they were not from our area.

We were anxious to get to Larroque as soon as we could so continued on our way passing everything in sight including numerous cars towing caravans and trailers. Many others had bicycles strapped to their roofs or on trailers. French drivers have some peculiar driving habits. They overtake leaving about six inches to spare and tend to leave their left indicators on all the time that they are in the fast lane, not just when they are passing. They do have one endearing habit – whenever a French driver coming in the opposite direction flashed his headlights at us it meant that we were approaching a police car and it was time to slow down. This signal invariably helped us because with such a long journey we could not afford to waste 12 hours on the road driving slowly. The French motorways are lovely to drive on, hardly any bends and always impeccably maintained. We have never yet seen road works on our numerous *autoroute* journeys.

It was fun pointing out familiar sights to my friend with the excitement mounting once we passed Bordeaux and were nearing home. The scenery certainly changed dramatically from the steep roofs that appeared to be slate rather than tile and walls of small dark grey stones of Brittany, to the flat Vendée with its unmistakable sharp odour of silage, then the pine forests approaching Bordeaux. We could tell when we were approaching Gascony by the gently rolling countryside with its vineyards, orchards and farmhouses tucked in among small woods. Dotted here and there were the tops of grand chateaux peeping over the trees. The other interesting feature about that drive was that we saw many cars with GB, German and Dutch plates on the earlier part of our journey but once past Bordeaux there were just French cars and one little GB Honda CRX carrying two French women – well, we did both own property in France after all, so classed ourselves as natives.

It was pleasing to see Kay's delighted reaction to our ancient farmhouse. She loved it, dirt and all and could hardly wait to help me tidy up. We cleaned the kitchen and front room floors and strode into the jungle armed with our gardening implements. Kay went for the vigorous jobs such as sawing overhanging branches and attacking the brambles with vigour. I felt a bit of topiary would improve the garden no end so created domes and spheres out of the laurel and box. When Kay started digging around the rose bushes and canna plants an unmistakable odour of sewage assailed our nostrils – so that was where the chamber pot used to be emptied! The roses did not seem to mind, they were flowering vigorously but the cannas looked unhappy and have never flowered in all the years we have had Larroque. Kay had brought some tomato plants that she had grown from seed and we planted those near the front wall of the house.

When it started getting dark we decided it was time to stop. Our efforts had made a huge difference to our view from the kitchen window. We now looked out between neatly pruned laurel spheres and rose bushes across the intervening fields to Janet's cluster of farm buildings. We had also cleared a path leading down from the clearing in front of the kitchen window to the chicken house on the lower level. It was time to eat. Corned beef and fried eggs with salad, washed down with a cup or two of good English tea constituted a perfectly good meal for campers. Kay's camping bed looked very comfortable next to my inflatable mattress but it did not seem fair to ask her to change places. We slept well in spite of the soft rustling and squeaking noises that seemed to surround us – from the ceiling and the walls.

The next day Kay and I spent a little time in our nearest town, had *café crême* and *tartes aux abricots* (apricot tarts) at the café that Phillip and I frequented then returned to say hello to the Boivins. Predictably, Marie informed us that we were having dinner with them because several family members from Paris were going to be there and we must meet them. We spent the rest of the afternoon taming the garden and wondered who the young man was who rode his noisy motorbike along the road that separated our property from Janet's, then along the main road, next along the narrow road to Marie's home and then, the last side of the square, along the road from Marie's home to Janet's. He came over to say hello, introducing himself as Laurent, and pointing vaguely in the direction of Janet's home. He spoke only French and asked (we think) why our husbands were permitting us to do such had work in the garden. We replied that they were not there to keep an eye on us, at least that's what we meant to say. He looked bewildered and left after a few minutes, roaring away on his motorbike. After another hectic few hours of gardening we cleaned up, prettied ourselves and drove back to Marie and Pierre's home.

We were greeted by Dominique's excited little cousins shouting *"les anglais, les anglais"* and directing us to another house across the road from Marie and Pierre. Dinner was to be held there as there were too many people to fit into Marie's kitchen. Several tables were laid along two sides of the room in an L-shaped fashion and there were at least 25 people there including the family we knew, Janet in her slippers and others who were introduced to us explaining the family relationships. We were confused to say the least but were seated next to Jean-Paul who was very witty and kept us in stitches all evening. The food was outstanding as usual – lots of sliced sausage and homemade *pâté* of several types, a beautifully arranged salad of neatly sliced avocado and tomato and barbecued quail for the main course. Marie and Dominique (and as many female relatives as were around) had spent hours that afternoon preparing the quail and slicing the potatoes for the *pommes frites*. Kay's French was better than mine but even she got words confused and declared that her head was a *mélange* (mixture) after a couple of glasses of wine. To this day neither she nor I know what she really meant to say. We were pleased to see that our contribution of a large shop-bought *tarte aux framboises* was enjoyed as much as the other desserts. Regretfully we said goodbye to the people we would not see again, good night to our old friends and left, not before promising to visit Janet's domain the next morning.

Janet's home, outbuildings and garden were as impeccable as her scrupulously neat fields, the total opposite of Larroque. She lived with her son, who farmed the land, in a beautifully renovated farmhouse. The garden was screened off from the fields by a row of conifers and surrounded by a white fence to keep the three dogs out.

Our arrival was heralded by a mad outbreak of loud barking and two enormous Alsatians and one dog of uncertain breed but apparently ferocious temper surrounded the car. Kay and I stayed put until Janet shouted at the dogs and they slunk off into the barn which was then firmly shut. Janet assured us it was safe to emerge and we sheepishly got out.

The garden was filled with masses of flowers. In the centre of the small, well-manicured lawn was a little well with a wooden cover and small roof. This too was overflowing with petunias of all hues.

The house was beautifully tiled and filled with lovingly polished antique furniture. Janet had been a widow for several years and owned several properties in addition to this one. Her

The flower-bedecked well in Janet's garden.

daughter Janine lived in one of the houses in Fleurance, a pretty town not too far away. Robert was out in the fields and we could see a small red speck that was a tractor moving back and forth in the distance. We told Janet we had met her son the day before when he was riding his motorbike and she laughed saying Robert only drove his tractor or his Audi. The young man we had met was Laurent, Janine's boyfriend.

There was a piano in the hall and a huge grandfather clock. The kitchen looked as though it had come straight out of *Homes and Gardens.* It had dark solid wood units and a gleaming quarry-tiled floor. The large fireplace which was the same size as the one in Larroque, had been tiled and now housed a modern cooker and microwave oven. The kitchen table was solid oak with matching chairs. Kay and I were invited to sit down and an *apéritif* offered. Packets of crisp tasty snacks were opened and we were urged to eat. Janet kept on saying what sounded like *"Allee-ze"* every time she pointed to the food and glasses. We could not find this in Larousse which we kept with us at all times and I wonder whether this was an Occitan word or one that Janet had invented.

We then had a tour of the house with its numerous bedrooms, a beautifully furnished dining room with another massive oak dining table covered with padded tablecloths and the attic where the cats lived because the dog of unknown ancestry had eaten one of them some years before. Kay and I looked at each other, thankful we had stayed in the car until the dogs were locked up. We were next shown the massive barns which housed the latest farming equipment imported from the U.K., some of the machines being as tall as a two-storey house. A tray of fresh eggs and several bags of plump garlic bulbs were pressed upon us before we left in spite of my pointing out that we had a small car with no extra space. Another generous French neighbour and friend! She made me promise to bring Phillip for dinner to meet Robert and Janine the next time we visited Larroque. We drove back past Marie's home where we stopped to say *"A bientôt"* (See you soon) rather than *"Au revoir"* (goodbye) because I knew I would be back with Phillip in a few weeks' time. We had more garlic forced upon us, this time from Marie's kitchen garden which kept her family and friends in fresh vegetables and salads throughout the growing season and bottled vegetables in winter.

Kay and I drove back to England with the car reeking of garlic but it was worth it as all our friends at work were thrilled to get fat bulbs of fresh garlic from France.

Towards the end of July we set sail for France once again, this time deviating from our usual overnight Portsmouth-Cherbourg ferry to an afternoon voyage to Caen. I felt exceedingly pleased with myself because I had telephoned the hotel in Caen and made the reservation all by myself (having written it all down first, courtesy of the phrases in Berlitz), even down to asking for a room with a shower (*douche*) rather than a bath. I had also asked for directions to the hotel and had been sent a map. Unfortunately the little map on the back of the hotel brochure did not specify which roads were one way but after circling the town a couple of times we accidentally came across the road we wanted and found the hotel. It was quite late by this time and the dining room was closed to add to Phillip's frustration so we set off to find a nearby restaurant. Just beside the hotel was a small café with a sign advertising *crêpes*. I discovered a new taste which soon became a favourite – pancakes with a sweet chestnut filling. This was not quite the steak that my carnivorous husband was hoping for but we were too tired to look for another eating place. We had been up early that morning and fitted in almost a full day's work before tearing down the A3 to the ferry so decided that bed was the best option.

The elderly couple who ran the café had a little dog which slept on a cushion beside the cash register. Every time a customer entered he would rise and go to meet the newcomer then retire to his cushion. A few years later we were in Caen again with a few hours to spare and decided to visit the 'Crêpes Café' as we called it. We could not see the little dog so asked the lady where he was. She was delighted we remembered him and said that he now preferred to have his cushion just outside the toilet door and refused to sleep anywhere else.

Larroque was welcoming with its blooming roses and the neat grassy area in front of the house and barn. Pierre had obviously been keeping our grass (which earlier in the month was more like hay) under control and had even cut the grass in our field. We took our presents, English chocolates this time, to Marie and Pierre and discovered that our local village *fête* was being held that night and we had to attend as we now were part of the village. Our village is about five minutes' drive away. It is very small with no shops apart from one that collects and distributes the local farmers' produce. There is a small, very old church, a cluster of stone houses and a *Mairie* which is open only three days a week. The Mayor had another job as well. Opposite the *Mairie* is a large barn-like building with a clearing on either side of it and this is where the *fête* is held each year at the beginning of August. We got there to find cars lining both sides of the road, a couple of stalls selling sweets and toys and a makeshift bar around which lounged our fellow villagers. We felt a bit conspicuous and self-conscious with our substandard French but were soon made to feel at home as Marie and Dominique introduced us to practically everyone as '*les anglais*'.

It was a swelteringly hot day and we sat on the grassy slope overlooking a large tank full of water with a tree trunk balanced across it. It seems there were two competing teams at the *fête* each year – the local village team and the team of firemen from a neighbouring village about five minutes' drive away. There were vociferous supporters for each side in the audience. The sport began with a member of each team balanced on the tree trunk wielding wet towels with which they attempted to knock each other off into the water. One by one each of the men fell in, sometimes without even being pushed off the log, possibly to cool off and the last survivor was cheered deafeningly by his team as they were the winners. Next there were various races for the wives, girlfriends and children from the two villages and lastly a tug of war between the male teams. We were pleased to see Pierre and Robert join the fray but the firemen showed they had more brawn than the farmers and our village gallantly conceded defeat.

In the meantime the local organising team including the Mayor, his wife and many others started the barbecue and arranged the tables, benches and chairs along three walls of the barn. There was a stage at one end where equipment had been set up and lively music filled the air. Marie had organised several seats for the family which included us and there were two spare seats which were being guarded zealously. We all sat down and were served by a host of helpers each wearing T shirts with the name of our village printed stylishly on the back. They were on sale so Phillip and I bought a couple and wear them religiously at least once each summer. There were little children wearing similar T shirts, who also helped by carrying paper plates with sliced French bread and by handing out the paper plates and cups for the eager diners. Laurent and his girlfriend Janine were among those waiting on the tables. Our two missing companions then appeared and were introduced as '*Monsieur le Boulanger et Madame la Boulangère*' rather than by their own names. They were late because they had to finish their baking before they could leave – France would not function if fresh bread was not available throughout the day! Their bakery was in the town that the firemen came from and they were congratulated heartily on the quality of the bread that had obviously ensured success.

The first course of *le diner* consisted of half a Gers melon with fragrant orange flesh containing a good quantity of *floc*. The melons were sweet but Marie said the ones her husband grew were even better. Plastic wine bottles were plonked down on the tables and the merriment began. The next course consisted of small pieces of some type of meat which was very chewy though tasty. Dominique said it was *'la volaille'* which according to the trusty Larousse meant poultry but this did not taste like normal chicken. Eventually we discovered that this was a great delicacy prepared from chicken and duck gizzards. Once again knowledge was not a good idea for me, I could not eat any more knowing what it was. Demands for more *'ping'* echoed round the room. Plates spilling over with chips were placed on the tables, bowls of sliced tomato appeared and the waiters brought large dishes containing steaks *(biftecks)* and steaming green beans. The helpings were huge but there were enough people with hearty appetites who were happy to help out. Bottles of red wine were replaced as soon as they were empty and we were urged to eat and drink not only by our friends at the table but by those waiting on the tables. Dessert was a slice of apricot tart and a fresh nectarine accompanied by a small glass of Armagnac. The mayor and his wife walked around the tables greeting all the people and welcomed us to the village, a charming touch.

No sooner had we finished eating than the tables were cleared and the seats turned around to face the stage where the M.C. was encouraging everyone to participate in the singing, musical instrument and poetry competition. People of all ages took part to thunderous applause. Phillip nipped out quickly for a breath of fresh air when it looked as though he was going to be petitioned to sing and I pleaded the after-effects of too much *vin*. The high point of the evening then began with a disco. The smallest children, some only two or three years old held hands and danced near the stage. Older ones pranced around in their own group. The teenagers and adults swung around merrily to the rhythm of familiar tunes. An octogenarian who, we were told, lived alone and looked forward each year to the *fêtes* of this and surrounding villages danced with many of the women in the room. Even I was not exempt. He danced very well with many twirls and flourishes holding himself ramrod straight and bowed low when the dance was over. Phillip and I could not resist the music of our youth and danced till we were about to drop. My elderly dancing companion waved goodbye as we left saying *"À l'année prochaine"* – till next year.

We spent the next few days toiling in the garden, sanding down and painting doors. Henri came to tell us that our builder was very busy and could not do any more work for us (we heard that he was busy constructing swimming pools for other, wealthier homeowners) and promised to send someone else who would be reliable. In the meantime, almost every morning when we opened the front door we would find a gift of some sort — a box of melons (Robert), or tomatoes and beans by the bagful (Marie), more melons (Pierre) and more tomatoes (Janet), eggs and garlic (Marie). They were amazed when we protested that we could not possibly eat all that they gave us as there were only the two of us. The reply was that we must eat more.

A return visit to the Pizzeria was a must. Cooking on our little gas camping stove meant that we could not have elaborate meals and there are only so many things one can do with a single ring — bacon, eggs and tomato cooked together, an omelette, scrambled eggs, sausages, lamb chops. We were quite happy with salad, cheese, and fresh *baguettes* for lunch but dinner was becoming a bit tedious. Phillip missed the curries I used to make at home in England and decided we should bring the ingredients with us on the next visit. I reminded him that we would also need separate rings for cooking the rice and lentils and could we please consider a nice Aga cooker which would not only cook but heat water and heat the whole house from what I had read. The only problem of course was the cost – approximately £8000 plus the cost of having it transported and a flat raised platform built for it, also the hotel bill for two nights for the two men who would install it. There were other possibilities, Rayburn cookers and an elegant French cooker in black and gold but the prices were still pretty steep. I realised this amount of money would go a long way towards renovating Larroque (once we had saved it up) and we decided to bring our Sunbeam Multicooker from England and to buy an electric two-ring table-top cooker the next time we went to the supermarket in Auch.

We were welcomed like long-lost friends by Michel at the Pizzeria and escorted to a table where Michel sat down and chatted with us about Larroque briefly. It was such a heart-warming feeling to be accepted as friends and neighbours by so many of the people we met from time to time. We eat at the Pizzeria every time we visit Larroque and are always greeted with the same enthusiasm. We have also made friends with the staff at one of the cafés in our local town where the pistachio ice cream is out of this world.

We thoroughly enjoyed our two weeks' stay in Larroque though it was still basically a campsite. We got accustomed to our inflatable mattress and did not mind the nightly routine of pumping it up because air had leaked out during the day. It was wonderful not having to wake up at 5.15am to prepare for the mad dash to work. Our deadline was 11am as we had to get to our *boulangerie* for our daily *baguette* or round loaf of *pain de campagne* before noon when it closed. Like many of our British friends who love France we too found the two-hour lunch period when every single shop was shut rather irksome, but learned to organise our lives around it. Though our French vocabulary was rapidly growing I still had problems with tenses, gender and numbers. At our local post office I asked for 14 stamps for postcards to England and thought they were quite expensive. It was only when I got home and checked that it dawned on me that I had asked for *"quarante timbres"* (40) instead of *"quatorze"* (14). Another problem arose with the word *"plus"*. We assumed it always meant more and could not understand that the lady at the *boulangerie* was saying there was **no more** bread, rather than there was more.

That first summer, washing our clothes by hand in a small basin with water heated over the stove was part of the fun, especially as everything dried within minutes in the fierce sun. My clothes line was strung up between the tall posts holding up the open barn. The thick stone walls kept the house cool and pleasant with the breeze blowing through the open windows and I spent most of the afternoon indoors. My outdoor efforts were mainly in the mornings, tidying up the garden, picking blackberries and chipping off the rendering on the front of the house. The effects were beginning to show and much of the lower part of the front wall of the house now had its lovely stone showing through. The topiary required some more attention and Kay's tomato plants with their tiny green tomatoes needed daily watering. I had found an old jug in the stable which did the job admirably. There were lots of old rusted pots (chamber pots possibly) and pans that we unearthed while toiling in the garden. One exciting find was what appeared to be a marble shell-shaped basin buried in the soil on the slope between the front clearing and the chicken house level below. Sadly it turned out to be just plaster which had been poured out over the slope and dried in the shape of a

An old lady sitting outside her house, shelling peas.

basin. A rusty old pot made a lovely container for a small trailing vine that I bought, knowing full well that it would not last once we left for home. Phillip preferred to roast in the sun (you would not believe he is a skin pathologist), coming in at intervals to pour cold water over himself. He did have a rather dashing tan even before the end of the two weeks. By 1pm the sun shone fiercely on the front of the house and, if we were eating a late lunch, Phillip's seat would be in front of the front door while mine would be in the hall, in the shade.

We enjoyed our drives around the countryside in the cool of the evening. After the almost complete silence of the sacred lunch break from about mid-day to 2pm, the shops would open again and cars would venture out onto the roads. It was fascinating to see neighbours sitting on chairs outside their front doors, gossiping or preparing vegetables for the evening meal.

We met our new *maçon,* a small, plump, energetic man called Yves and his wife Anne-Marie. We explained what we wanted done in the house: the roof, new floors, the walls, new ceilings, the rest of the rendering removed from the front of the house, the walls repointed, the musty, woodworm-ridden cupboards removed, the fireplaces cleaned up and an arched opening put in between the room adjacent to the kitchen and the room with the bread oven. Fortunately Anne-Marie spoke a little English so we felt confident that she had transmitted our wishes to her husband, but were careful to say that we would fax them the details in French once we got home and could we please then have an estimate.

This time we varied our routine on the way home, leaving Larroque at noon instead of at sunrise, and spending the night in a charming hotel at Comburg before the morning crossing to England and work.

Chapter Six

November in the Gers

Our Guildford Adult Education Classes started in September. The previous year I had joined a course on watercolour painting and enjoyed it tremendously. This year I enrolled for French classes and was advised to join the intermediate group rather than the beginners' one, thanks to Reader's Digest and Berlitz 'French on the Move'. We met once a week from 7–9pm at the local school. Those of us who got there early helped arrange the seats in a semicircle as the tutor preferred an informal setting. The worst part of moving the desks was the disgusting lumps of dried chewing gum stuck under the tables – one knew instantly that this was school property!

There were about 12 in the class ranging from young adults to one couple in their late sixties. Some of the group owned homes in France, the others all wanted to either work in France or buy property there. Our tutor, a kind and gentle man who obviously loved France and everything French, used to teach A-level French before he retired. He was patient yet firm with us ensuring that we got as much as we could out of the classes. I found it hard going, especially listening to the tapes that accompanied our textbook. The dialogue was so fast that the words seemed to merge into one another and were incomprehensible until I could see them in the text book. I have always found it much easier to understand written French than the spoken language, especially with all the different accents. The course was extremely useful, reinforcing what I was studying myself at home, especially as I was now learning the correct pronunciations.

At the beginning of November I had to attend a scientific meeting in Houston, Texas. One free afternoon was all it took for me to indulge in one of my wild ideas. I had been thinking about curtains for Larroque for some months now although it was obvious that there was a lot of major renovation to be done before the finer aspects of civilisation could be considered. Having wandered through the stores in Guildford I discovered that I would have to spend a fortune on curtain material and that was not feasible. However, in Houston my colleague (and friend) Barbara and I discovered Woolworths with its vast array of household goods at ridiculously cheap prices. I went mad and bought many yards of pretty flowered material (I had measured the windows in summer so knew exactly how much was needed) with extra for a bedspread and cushions. There were also irresistible cotton rugs and huge balls of crochet cotton at giveaway prices. By the time I had filled my trolley I realised I would have to buy another suitcase to transport all these purchases. That was no problem, Woolworths had a cheap, expanding case which was perfect and I went home with extra luggage, eager to start on the new curtains.

Phillip and I decided on a long weekend in Larroque at the end of November. Yves had sent us an estimate for all the work we wanted done and had mentioned vital improvements such as guttering because the rooms were damp and musty and there was no damp course so he would have to dig a trench around the whole house and perhaps drain the pond. He had also discovered woodworm in all the old beams, in the parquet flooring in the front room and, worse still, termites in the stone walls. This was quite a blow as the repairs and extermination of the unwanted inhabitants were very expensive. We talked to our bank manager, decided to scrimp on luxuries and borrowed the money for essential repairs. Yves promised to start straight away, tackling the termites first.

When we drove up to Larroque in late November it was dry and cool and the sun was shining. All the wood in the house had been treated with a special paint on the surface and with some solution that was injected into the wood. Similar inroads had been made into the walls. We found it hard to understand how termites could attack thick stone walls until it was pointed out that it was the material between the stones that was crumbling. The house smelled strongly of anti-woodworm solution and there was even more powdery stuff and dust on the floor. The two front rooms had had their wood floors and ceilings removed because they were untreatable and there was a film of mildew on the plaster of the walls. It was all quite depressing. However, the kitchen looked much better now that the old cupboards had been removed, also the outer creaking door. The inner part of the long hall had now become part of the kitchen, separated from the front half by a door. The huge fireplace in the kitchen had been cleaned up; most of the thick lining of soot had been removed as had the old black wooden mantelpiece, leaving only the huge beam that supported the upper part of the fireplace. The kitchen walls had been treated with *enduit rustique,* a rough coating, rather than plaster as Yves said it would help prevent damp. The walls looked a lovely pale cream but there were little deposits of granular material (saltpetre we were told) on the floor. These deposits became something we got accustomed to clearing up every time we visited Larroque for several years afterward.

However, there was only earth in place of the hall and kitchen floors. Yves said that so many of the tiles in the hall were broken that he could not find enough intact ones to match up. Also, he had tried to save the kitchen tiles but the roots of the grapevine on the south-facing wall of the kitchen were coming up through the tiles, so the grapevines and the roses along the south-facing wall were uprooted and discarded. He also had to replace the supporting beam over the doorway between the kitchen and the adjacent room (which was going to be our dining room). He knew that we were photographing the various stages of renovation so had taken a lot of pictures for us including the first hole in the wall between the dining room and the bread oven room that would eventually become the arched opening. It was obvious we could not spend even one night with all the dust and other debris so we handed over the money we owed Yves and drove to our friends Sylvie and Armand yet again for a comfortable, dust-free bedroom.

The next day was bright and sunny again so we decided to see a bit more of our surroundings and drove to the Pyrenées. An hour later we were driving up the foothills towards the snow-covered peaks. It was warm enough to have the top off the car until we reached the snow. We could see small shepherds' huts dotted at intervals in the distance with no signs of civilisation between. Time to go back. The road was so narrow in parts that it was quite frightening especially as the driver (me this time) was very near the edge of the road and there were no walls or fences keeping us away from the steep slopes. We decided to celebrate our safe return to the normal flat straight roads of France by stopping at the first restaurant we saw for a filling lunch. We had a hearty vegetable soup with warm French bread, followed by a rabbit stew for Phillip and a tasty omelette with diced chorizo sausage for me.

On the way back we decided to say "hello" to the Boivins. As we approached their home a tantalising aroma wafted over our nostrils. We drove into a hive of activity. A huge iron pot was bubbling over an outdoor brick oven-cum-barbecue. Sticking out of the pot was a pig's head, ears and all. The pot, which was stirred at intervals by various female family members, also contained carrots and onions in addition to various spices. Marie laughed at our amazement and told us that this was how *pâté de tête* was prepared and promised to save us a jar or two. The pig had been slaughtered and carved into the various traditional bits by the local *boucher* (butcher) and Anna and various other cousins had come to help with preparing potted meats with the smaller scraps. I am not quite sure what happened to the feet, perhaps they too were in the pot as no part of the pig is wasted in France. The Boivins and many of the farming families in our region were self-sufficient as far as food is concerned. They were by no means rich people and they worked very hard summer and winter. The menfolk toiled in the fields and the income was dependent on the price paid for the crop each year. The women grew their own salad ingredients and vegetables and bottled the excess for winter. Chickens, ducks and quail were reared from day-old chicks, in season. *M. le Boulanger* brought fresh bread in his van daily and often was bullied into staying for a bite to eat. In return for allowing him to use our open barn to store his hay, Pierre cut our grass for us (this was not a lawn by any stretch of the imagination, just overgrown grass encroaching on the clearing in front of the house). He often ploughed our bit of land as well to get rid of the weeds. We insisted that they harvest all our pears and figs as we were never at Larroque when the fruit ripened and Marie gave us some of the lovely jam she made with our fruit. The one berry she did not use however, was sloes. I resolved to gather some the next autumn to make sloe gin – a family favourite.

On Sunday we decided to go to the ancient church in another nearby *bastide* (old fortified village) to attend a Gregorian mass (*messe*). The little church was packed out and we were squeezed in between two fairly large ladies who conversed with each other over our heads – a difficult feat as Phillip is very tall and they were quite short. Hearing us speak to each other in English, a lady behind us leaned forward and introduced herself, handing us a business card which said she was Lady Marie-Claire Howard. She explained that she was married to an English lord who preferred to live in France now that he was retired and invited us to tea whenever we were free. Unfortunately we did not have a telephone at Larroque so never took Lady Marie-Claire up on her invitation. The Gregorian mass was moving although we did not understand a word.

One year we decided to spend Christmas at Larroque just to see how it was celebrated in Gascony. The children flatly refused to accompany us as they had been invited to parties and other exciting evenings out. We had to open all the presents early at home before we left for France. We promised the children a proper Christmas lunch on New Year's Day so the Christmas turkey was sitting in the freezer at home. We took food with us in case all the shops were closed in our town.

Most of the streets there had pretty lights strung across at intervals. The trees along the main street were decorated with square parcels wrapped in shiny paper and tied up with bright ribbons. We wondered what would happen to them should it rain. Larroque was cold but we had bought a large portable gas heater – the type that runs on bottled gas – and moved it to whichever room we were in. It did not feel like Christmas as we had neither a tree nor decorations and the children were not there (even though they normally only appear for Christmas breakfast of scrambled eggs with smoked salmon, open their presents and then disappear to catch up on their beauty sleep, reappearing when Christmas lunch is ready.

I had baked two Christmas cakes that year, one for the family to share when we had our belated Christmas feasting, one for the Boivins. They seemed slightly taken aback at this gift, probably as French gateaux are light and look different and they were not sure what this fruit-filled offering was, even though it reeked of rum. In fact, Marie was busy mixing cocoa and *farine* (flour) to make their traditional Yule log when we arrived. We suspect they did not like the fruit cake but were too polite to say so. It was always difficult to know what to take as presents; apparently it is insulting to take a bottle of wine when invited for a meal to a French home. Happily, friends back home in the U.K. were always pleased to receive a gift of French wine or cheese so that was never a problem.

We decided it would be nice to attend the carol service at our local cathedral as it is such a beautiful building and we thought we could sing the carols even if we did not understand the service. The cathedral was freezing cold and the benches were very hard. The service was very different from what we were used to and we did not recognise a single one of the carols. Nevertheless it was an uplifting experience. On the way home we encountered a lot of ground fog which made driving along the narrow unlit roads really difficult. Phillip took it all in his stride and got us home safely but the house was cold and we had to snuggle up to the heater to get warmed up. We decided that we would not spend Christmas at Larroque again until we had a proper heating system installed and a cooker so that we could be comfortable. Naturally, we hoped the children would join us then.

On several occasions we have spotted deer in the woods near our village. They have never ventured into our own wood as far as we know but neither have we, not even to look for truffles, as it is so dense and impenetrable. One of the nearby farms has a herd of Charolais cattle with pale colouring and large liquid eyes. They wander up to the fence and stand perfectly still while Phillip photographs them, on virtually every trip we make to France. Speaking of cows, I cannot remember noticing fresh milk sold in supermarkets in France – we only seem to be able to get bottled long-life milk around Larroque. Perhaps most of the cows' milk gets made into cheese. We have wanted for a long time to visit the caves where the Roquefort ewes' cheese is made but have never been able to find the area. Obviously the family navigator needs to brush up her skills!

On one of our trips to Larroque we decided to drive through the Loire valley and visited the village of the Troglodytes, a charming place where most of the houses are caves within the hills. The front room is the only conventionally built room in each house, the other rooms being underground. We have not yet had the opportunity to see the inside of one of these intriguing homes.

We were dismayed and embarrassed to hear an account of Dominique's school trip to the U.K. She and a friend went to Scotland for a week to stay with the family of a girl their age. Not only did the family not speak any French, they did not speak to the girls in English either. The Scottish schoolgirl spent her free time with her own friends and Dominique and Eve were left to their own devices. They did get taken to see a castle one day. Most evenings they had to eat dinner by themselves at the kitchen table and they did not care much for the food either. What a contrast to the French hospitality we have experienced, although this was probably an exceptional case.

Once back home in England I set to work in earnest on the curtains for Larroque, blue for our bedroom as I had plenty left over to make a fitted bedspread and pink for the guest bedroom. I also started crocheting old-fashioned lace curtains for the new open doorway between the kitchen and the little inner hall which led to the bathroom and toilet and for the other open doorway between the same hall and the bread oven room which at that time was destined to be the sitting room. This was the extent of our do-it-yourself expertise. Phillip was forbidden to attempt any DIY in Larroque, not only because of lack of time but because of past experience with his handiwork a few years before. We had just moved into our home in Guildford and had a white Siamese kitten called Snowy belonging to Kathryn, our elder daughter and a floppy, very young tan and white cocker spaniel called Shandy, who belonged to Sharon, the younger daughter. Fortunately Stephen, the eldest, was more into BMX bikes and these lived in the garage and did not have to be fed and watered. We decided a cat flap was eminently desirable as I seemed to be landed with litter tray duties and Phillip offered to install one in the kitchen door. The children and I stayed out of the way as thumbs seemed to be hammered with monotonous regularity, accompanied by much loud swearing and cursing. We only ventured into the kitchen when we heard a triumphant shout of "Come and see what a brilliant job I've done!" The cat flap was neatly in place until the kitten decided to try it out. Immediately the part of the door below the flap fell out and both the kitten and the pup decided that was a much quicker way to get in and out, leaving the cat flap as decoration. The fact that it was freezing outside and a gale blew through the opening in the door did not endear my poor husband to the rest of the family. Any item that had to be assembled at home usually resulted in extreme irritability because most instructions are not written in plain English and all the little component parts have strange names that we have never heard of before. So Phillip was let off any work on Larroque apart from sanding and painting, both of which he did with expertise.

This explains why Yves became so essential to us. He was not only a first-rate builder, he had a feel for old buildings and restored everything in the traditional fashion. He was as thrilled as we were when he showed us the ancient stones that formed the fireplace in the dining room – they had carved writing on them stating that they had once been part of a chateau in our village. This no longer exists so we feel we own at least part of a château. Yves restored the bread oven to perfection, even tiling its domed roof and knew exactly what I had in mind when I suggested an arched opening between the dining room and bread oven room. He is also a landscape designer and gardener and we have great plans for him when Larroque is fully restored — with his help my dream of a Monet's garden lookalike will become a reality one day when we are living in France.

Chapter Seven

Le Pâques au Gers

We started collecting old furniture for Larroque, and any furniture we replaced such as our three-piece suite, was stored for France. We bought a second-hand dining table and chairs because we wanted to invite our French friends to our home for a change, once it was in a fit state.

In the meantime our friends in England were amazed at our persistence, having seen pictures of Larroque as it really was. I would look at the various rooms and see them the way they would look when the renovation was complete. The compliment I value most came from one of my colleagues: "When Grace says she is going to do something, no matter how far-fetched, she will not give up until she has done it." Half price sales with an additional discount at our local kitchen show-room meant we were able to buy lovely chestnut units for our second home. I had spent many hours with a plan of the kitchen drawn to scale on graph paper designing exactly how I wanted the units placed. As it was a large kitchen, about 18 ft by 18 ft (I have never got to grips with the metric system), we could place units along two of the walls and a peninsula unit along a third side. The fourth wall contained the 8-foot wide fireplace. There would be ample space for a small kitchen table and four chairs on the one side and space for the refrigerator on the other side of the peninsula unit between it and the door to the hall. We could not have wall-mounted cabinets as the walls were not straight; however we had lots of floor units and plenty of worktops. A wide shelf at worktop level would conceal the washing machine and dishwasher once we could afford them. The fireplace would accommodate the new cook-er and the recess facing the door to the hall would house a tall cabinet. We sent copies of the assembly instructions to Yves so he could pore over the diagrams (the instructions were in English, of course) well before the units arrived.

The floors at Larroque had been laid and the dining room now had its arched opening into the bread oven room accord-ing to the latest bulletin from France so it was now time for our next visit. We had never spent Easter in France so this would be a good opportunity to see how it was celebrated there. The boxes of kitchen units were stacked up in our garage next to the other bits of furniture collected for Larroque, squeezed in beside two BMX bikes, bits of other bicycles, an old car engine (all Steve's possessions), a ladder, two lawnmowers and vari-ous garden tools. We hired a diesel van and decided to take the Portsmouth-Bilbao ferry which in theory would mean a short-er drive at the France end although we would have to spend two nights on the ferry. It also meant we would see a bit of Spain and this was an added bonus to us seasoned travellers. We packed the van with a large wardrobe, dining table, six chairs, several boxes of kitchen units, two bedside tables, a couple of boxes of paperback books, our old three-piece suite and loads of cushions. We also added a new mop as the old one had worn out with use on the ancient kitchen and hall tiles. As the wardrobe was empty, I stuffed a spare duvet and bed linen, clothes which could be used for toiling in the garden and house, spare shoes and Wellington boots into it. Our briefcases had to fit in as well because Phillip was working on a textbook and I had a chapter to complete for a textbook by the end of April and I had to take a microscope to review scores of Pathology slides. There was also room for a spade, fork and a new saw. We had to enlist the help of Steve and his many friends as the boxes and furniture were too heavy for me to be of any help loading the van.

We set off in great excitement in spite of the fact that we were perched up on high uncomfortable seats in the van rather than in one of our cars and the diesel engine was very noisy. I absolutely refused to help with the driving, never having driven a van before. After our usual enjoyable dinner on board the ferry we repaired to our very comfortable cabin to do a bit of work before retiring for the night. All was well until the next morning when I attempted to get out of bed and felt violently seasick. The boat was being rocked vigorously and my stomach did not like it one bit. It was nothing like the gentle motion of the waves on our usual Channel crossing. What made things worse was the fact that Phillip was bright and alert after a good night's sleep, ready for a big breakfast. The very mention of bacon and eggs added to my misery and I begged to be left alone to die. Half an hour later Phillip brought me some weak tea and a slice of toast insisting I had to have it to feel better and he was absolutely right. I felt much better as the day wore on but could not face the dining room until the next day. We had managed to do quite a bit of work at sea so the time was not entirely wasted. Nevertheless we were pleased to dock at Santander and get on to firm land once more.

The drive to Pau through Spain was not much fun. The road wound up and down hills and the van chugged along at one of two speeds – slow and very slow. The Spanish police at the border were more suspicious than their French counterparts and insisted on inspecting the contents of the van. The French police were happy to see the documents that showed we owned property in France and waved us through quickly. The one other memory we have of that drive is the frequent smell of sewage that assailed our nostrils. About seven hours later we had passed Pau and Tarbes where we branched off north towards our much-loved Gascony. We arrived to find the clearing in front of the house a mire as it had rained a lot the previous week. Discarded building materials including plaster, cement, heaps of sand and bits of wood (many of them with malicious-looking large rusty nails sticking out) lay scattered on what we liked to refer to as our courtyard. I stepped down from the van and got stuck in the mud, leaving my shoe behind when I took a step. We entered the house to find it covered with dust, plaster and mouse droppings, not to mention spider webs. I burst into tears as this was such an anticlimax. Nevertheless, after sweeping up all the debris and washing the floors several times we were able to calm down and enjoy our house. The quarry-tiled floors were beautiful, a lovely pinkish brown, the dining room was bright and looked huge with its arched opening into the bread oven room.

We decided to leave unloading the van for the next day hoping that the ground would be a bit drier then. Luck was on our side – we were able to get all the furniture out of the van and into the house after it was thoroughly cleaned, just the two of us staggering under the weight. I have to admit that Phillip did the backbreaking portion of the lifting. It was fun unpacking and sorting out where everything should go. Now of course our dining table and chairs looked far too small for the huge dining room. We arranged the sitting room furniture in the dining room and used the dining table as a desk in the bread-oven room to accommodate the microscope and hundreds of slides that had to be read as part of a project during this holiday. The jute rugs I had bought on sale at Heals had seemed very large in the store but here they were dwarfed by the size of the rooms. I had also bought a beautiful handmade rug in beige and shades of blue and this looked just right in the bread-oven room. Our portable radio cum CD player was switched on and music resounded throughout the house. We had a wide selection of music ranging from Dire Straits to Fauré's Requiem and boxes of books to fill our leisure time. The curtains could not be hung as the rods had yet to be put up (by Yves as Phillip certainly did not have either the inclination or the right tools for drilling into the stone wall) but Larroque felt like home at last. The bed ordered by Sylvie arrived that afternoon: we were relieved not to have to pump up the inflatable mattress any more.

As we had brought so much work with us we decided to work in the mornings (at books, chapters and at the microscope) and go out in the afternoons. The garden was a mess again but there was nothing we could do until all the building rubble had been cleared. There was still work to be done on the house including repairing the holes in the attic floor, painting the doors and exposed beams with a protective solution which also coloured them a rich shade of brown. We felt this could all wait until the two-week summer break. There was a thunderstorm that second night and I was woken by the sound of water dripping onto the ceiling above our bed. This was accompanied by scuffling and scraping sounds which were quite terrifying in the depths of the countryside. Phillip, as always, slept soundly through all the noise and could not be roused to investigate the attic. The next morning we saw the holes in the roof where the rain came through but did not see any signs of life apart from some dung which was too small for a cat but too large for mice. We were later told that owls were responsible — that reassured us about the scuffling noises.

Marie and Pierre were delighted to see us as usual. We took a set of English bone china mugs as our Easter gift and were immediately offered *pastis* in them. It was very encouraging when, after listening to my account of the voyage across, Pierre remarked that I had made progress with my French. We were relieved to hear that business would be as usual in all our local shops (open on Good Friday, Easter Saturday, Easter Sunday morning and closed on Easter Monday). We needed to deposit money in the bank for the next few months' mortgage. Early on we had discovered how expensive it was and still is, to transfer money from the U.K. to France. At an average of £19.00 per transaction it made sense to send across as much money as we could afford each time. We then decided to take French francs in cash each time we visited Larroque. The time involved in separating the various denominations of notes, counting and labelling them was fair exchange for the hefty charges we were saving.

As our mortgage was with the Société Générale branch in Angoulême we thought it would be better to open another account with the branch in our local town and get them to transfer the mortgage payment to Angoulême every month. I got all our papers out, enlisted the help of Larousse and painstakingly wrote out all our instructions in French because there was no way I would be able to say it off the top of my head. We had not learned to think in French so had to translate everything we wanted to from English to French, stumbling over the grammar. Armed with this vital sheet of paper we drove to the bank and asked the cashier at the front desk whether we could see the manager. The cashier had got to know us by this time as we had deposited money there before, to be transferred to Angoulême. He, as always, was the essence of charm, asking whether we were *en vacances* and enquiring how the renovation was proceeding. He told us that he lived in a small village very near ours and recommended a trip there to see the ancient monastery and gardens. This to us is one of the most endearing aspects of France, at least the area we feel part of – the people we meet take the time to chat and seem to be really interested in us as individuals. Every time we go into a restaurant the other diners always nod and say *"Bonjour"*, a custom that is much more welcoming to strangers than the disinterest we were accustomed to back home.

The bank manager came out to usher us into his glass-walled office with its impeccably neat desk and computer. We did enquire as to whether he spoke any English but he replied, *"Je suis désolé"* – I am sorry – and went on to say that his wife taught English at a school in another town, but the only other language he spoke was Spanish. Anyway, I produced my sheet of paper explaining that my French was pretty bad so I had to write down what we needed. He then proceeded to read my instructions very carefully, looked up and asked who had written them. I confessed that I had done it all myself with the help of a dictionary. He nodded and then made a few grammatical corrections with a mischievous grin, saying it was very good and that he understood it all. Phillip joined in the spirit of the game and wrote '5/10' at the top of the sheet. *"Non, non"* said *Monsieur le Directeur* and changed the mark to 9/10. He then went on to say that the transaction would be sorted out and that eventually we might be able to transfer our mortgage to his branch from the one at Angoulême. He too could not understand why our mortgage had been arranged at that branch and we could not explain that we were so relieved to be given a mortgage at the time that we could not have cared less whether it came from a bank at the South Pole.

We had our *espresso* (Phillip) and *café crème* (me) at our usual café after buying a gateau to take with us to the Boivins for dinner that night. We were thrilled to be remembered by the assistant at the *boulangerie,* the same lady who, many months before, had pointed to the various types of French bread telling us their names: *baguette, ficelle, pain de campagne.* The cakes were beautifully decorated and there were even more varieties of chocolates in small boxes for the Easter season. The *droguerie* (hardware store) that we frequented was nearby and we dropped in, again to a warm welcome, to buy some mouse poison. It seemed a shame to have to do this but we now had furniture in Larroque and we did not want to find it wrecked by the wildlife. From the size of the droppings Yves had guessed that the unwelcome visitors were field mice which came in via the roof and he had advised to scatter the poison around the bottom of the rickety stairs before we left for home. We also bought the wood varnish that was supposed to treat any remaining woodworm, at an exorbitant price.

On our afternoon excursions we discovered many beautiful little hamlets and villages that soon became favourite haunts over the years. Our bank cashier's village was about 10 minutes' drive from Larroque. The village square or *place* was bordered by the walls of the ancient church on one side, stone houses on another, all of which had sculpted cats reclining on the windowsills and in nooks in the walls. Facing these houses was another set of stone houses, these with a covered, stone-floored *terrasse* (terrace). The first three of these houses had been converted into a hotel-restaurant. Tables and chairs were laid out on the terrace with welcoming blackboards on which were scribbled '*Crêpes'.* No second invitation was needed. We thought coffee and pancakes especially those with chestnut puree and Armagnac after visiting the *église* would be a nice way to round off the afternoon. The young girl from the office opposite the church unlocked the huge wrought-iron gates for us so that we could enter the walled garden which was immaculate, cool and serene. The church was at the opposite side of the garden, reached by a covered walkway paved with stone. It was a small, well-maintained church with a tiny, twisting staircase in one corner, barely the width of a person, leading to the roof where the views were fantastic. I felt quite claustrophobic climbing the narrow stone stairs which were worn with the tread of thousands of feet, clinging to the wall as I struggled up. It was not an experience I would want to repeat personally, though Phillip thought it was great. It was a relief to flop down on a seat in the little café and enjoy the space around us.

The coffee was good and the *crêpes* delicious but rather small and thin. We could easily have eaten six each. It was while we were relaxing over our coffee that an incident occurred which made us realise that perhaps French people are not all necessarily good and kind. Two women hikers wandered in and sat at the table next to ours. They ordered coffee and when they had finished one asked the waiter where the toilet was (I still remember the first time in France that I asked directions to the toilet and said, *"Où est la toilette, s'il vous plait?"* and the young waitress corrected me saying *"Où sont les toilettes"* – I hadn't minded one bit) and disappeared into the restaurant. The other hiker walked up to the display of printed skirts and scarves hanging on a rail, picked one up, held it against herself for size and then walked back to her table and stuffed it into her rucksack. When her friend returned they asked how much they owed for the coffee, paid and walked off. We couldn't believe that apparently well-to-do people would do something like that. We wondered whether we should alert the waiter but, in view of our limited vocabulary, decided against it. Although they were speaking French they could have been from another country, or so we hoped, because we did not want to spoil our image of France.

We also discovered a store on the outskirts of our local town that sold every type of household item one could desire, from solid pine and oak furniture to crockery, rugs, toys and garden furniture. We bought a plastic table and six chairs with a large parasol for our alfresco meals in summer as we now had the van in which to transport them, also a set of pretty blue china sideplates and flowered glasses. On the way home we passed a pine furniture store which also sold antiques and dropped in just to have a look. We could not resist buying a secondhand small square solid oak table for the kitchen as the dining table would be too big for the available space once the kitchen was installed. We then decided that a couple of French chairs with rush seats would be nice for our respective desks back home in Guildford and also threw in a nest of four solid oak side tables. The prices were amazingly cheap compared with those in good furniture stores in the U.K. The outdoor furniture would look good on our *terrasse* once it was built and the small oak table was perfect for our kitchen, with two of our own seats.

The roads between towns and villages in our area of France have no streetlights but do have extremely good warning arrows on all the sharp bends to reflect headlights, making night driving safe. We also noticed small red triangles or circles on posts marking driveways, again a bonus in the dark. We thought this would be a good idea for our drive and tried to describe what we were looking for at our local hardware store. The owner directed us to a bicycle shop where we were given bicycle reflector lamps. This was not quite what we had in mind, especially as we could see no way of attaching them to the metal posts identifying our driveway. However, a couple of years later we noticed proper red triangles attached to our posts and assume this was the work of our local *Mairie*.

The trip back to Santander was uneventful apart from the

same sewage odours we had experienced on our outward journey. We had to open up the back of the van again for the Spanish police who seemed perplexed that we needed a van to transport two rush-seated chairs but, as we could not speak each other's language they let us through eventually. It was good to return home to our creature comforts but we could not wait to get back to our beloved Larroque in summer knowing the kitchen units would have been installed and we could invite our friends to dinner for a change.

Chapter Eight
Squatters at Larroque

July arrived at last. We had collected more cushions, furniture and kitchen utensils to take to France with us as we would be spending three weeks there this time and wanted to feel at home.

The children could not understand why we were so excited about spending our time working on an ancient farmhouse when we had a lovely comfortable home in Guildford. There was no way we could persuade them to accompany us although we were a bit unsure about leaving them to their own devices at home. They had lots of friends who seemed to spend most of their leisure time in our home and we were worried that they would all move in the minute we set off for the ferry. The youngest, Sharon, was eighteen so they were perfectly capable of looking after themselves but we had reason to be concerned. When my father passed away in 1989 the children (aged 13 to 17) had to be left on their own at short notice for about four days. On arriving in New Orleans for the funeral I telephoned home (it was about midnight in Guildford) to make sure everything was all right. A strange male voice answered the phone and quickly passed it over to Steve when I asked suspiciously "Who is that?" I could hear loud music in the background and was not particularly reassured when Steve said everything was O.K., they just had a few friends over. It was not until we got back when our next-door neighbour who was a dear friend said we had such well brought–up children that I discovered the truth. On further questioning Jill, I discovered that Steve had gone to see her and the neighbours on the other side of us to ask whether they would mind him and his sisters holding a party that night. Of course they did not mind but apparently the house was full of youngsters and the music was pretty loud inside and out as they also had a barbecue in the garden. Steve later admitted to us that they had moved all the furniture out of the sitting room, rolled up the Chinese rug and locked away all the good china before the guests arrived. Nothing was damaged except one of the wall lights and to this day we have not been told how that happened.

Jill and Geoff, our neighbours on one side, and Jean and Leslie on the other, are wonderful people. The day we moved into our home in Guildford, a cold snowy day in January, trays of tea, coffee and cakes arrived for the removal men and us from the neighbours on either side. This was even before they had met us! They were exceptionally tolerant of the noise made by our three teenagers and their numerous friends. The youngsters also ran out of food the day after the party and had to borrow money from Jill the next day. They were all older now and more responsible so we did not have too many qualms about leaving them on their own but I gave them only the first week's groceries money and hid the next two lots saying I would telephone from France when they were due to go shopping. Once bitten, twice shy!

We arrived at Le Havre at 7.30am and began the long drive to Gers. There were traffic jams at several places along our route, possibly because it was Saturday, July 30th and the beginning of the French summer holiday. At Poitiers we decided to find an alternative route and left the motorway with its bad-tempered drivers tooting their horns at the slightest provocation, meandering our way down towards Bordeaux. The weather was stiflingly hot and the sun shone straight onto our heads as the sun-roof was open. Phillip got his tan even before we reached our home. Perhaps we would have been wiser to have stayed on the *autoroute* as we did not arrive at Larroque until midnight. The latter part of the drive had been quite pleasant driving past fields of bright red poppies and the perfectly straight rows of grapevines with their new green leaves. On our last visit all the vineyards had skeleton vines that had been drastically pruned leaving just one leading shoot. The evening breeze was cool and once it grew dark there were hundreds of small flying insects hell-bent on suicide, hurling themselves against the windscreen.

We missed seeing the familiar landmarks near home. Once past the little village to the east of us we always pass what we call Sleeping Beauty's house – a house invisible from the road as it was surrounded by a screen of 15 foot high conifers. Next we would see a tall beacon in the distance on the left, probably a television and radio transmitter, then Janet's reservoir, next our woods on the left and then a little crossroads sign just in front of our turning. We always felt very pleased that our little road was actually signposted as was the next one down, the narrow road to the Boivins' home. The smaller roads have no street lights and we saw none of our landmarks but managed to recognise our woods and turned into our own little road and drive. We thought again that we should try to buy the reflecting triangles or circles which are so common at the entrance to French farmhouse driveways. Once night falls, in that part of the country at least, all the shutters are closed and there is total darkness except for the occasional chink of light that escapes through a broken shutter. It is impossible to tell whether anyone is at home or not.

This time our courtyard was dry, all the building rubbish had been cleared away and the *terrasse* had been laid around the front and side of the house. There was also a little stone wall around the part of the terrace to the left of the front door with a stone *jardinière* built next to it for plants. The stones Yves had used, *pierres du Lot,* were gleaming in the headlights and were beautiful shades of pale gold, cream, white and pale pink, we discovered the next day. We opened the front door to find hordes of small, bright green winged creatures in the hall and in our beautiful new kitchen, in the dining and sitting rooms. Fortunately the bedroom door had been shut and there was no visible insect life there. The bathroom and toilet doors were also shut and those two rooms were also insect–free. We dumped our cases in the bedroom, shut the door firmly, hurriedly made the bed and got in thinking that it would be wiser to look around the house in daylight.

The next morning we discovered that the shield-shaped bright green insects were not the only squatters. We had pretty green frogs sitting on the horizontal pieces of wood that held the shutters of the kitchen window together, four on each piece. When we opened the shutters they leapt off, changing from their 2 inch sitting size to about eight inches with their hind legs stretched out. We then discovered another one of their family sitting in the shower. There were clumps of strange, small black insects in the kitchen and dining room, mouse droppings in both fireplaces and about ten dead field mice lying in various positions near the staircase. They had evidently enjoyed the grain coated with bright pink poison and were paying the penalty. I felt quite sorry for the pretty little creatures at first then discovered that they had eaten large holes in every cushion of the three-piece suite. What was even worse was that they had managed to make their way through the plastic covering the rolled-up beige and blue rug, had eaten a large hole in it and also peed on it to add insult to injury. I resolved to put down double the dose of mice poison when we left for home. When we opened the shutters in the bread oven room there was a sudden rush of wings and a couple of bats flew out of the bread oven. We were really pleased we had not wandered through the house the previous night. I decided to check our brand new mailbox that was now sitting on the little wall at the edge of the *terrasse*, and noted the key would not turn but the door was unlocked yet stiff. I stuck my hand into the slit and yanked the door open, then screamed as I saw a small wasps' nest inside. Fortunately I did not get stung. By this time we had another visitor who seemed to know his way around – a very large Alsatian pup who was friendly but frighteningly big. He kept running around the house and would not leave when I said "Go". Then, in a sudden burst of inspiration I shouted *"Allez"* and off he went to his home next door. Phillip bravely ventured up into the attic not knowing what we would find next but there was no more wild life, only more piles of owl droppings.

We loved the kitchen, it looked exactly the way I had envisaged it with the peninsula unit, marble-effect work surface, brass rods and the typically French yellow and blue flowered splash-back tiles. We had no washing machine or dishwasher, nor a refrigerator – a necessity in this weather as we were staying three weeks. The Boivins had thoughtfully left us an old one of theirs but it probably did not like the journey to our house and refused to work. The curtain rods were up and all we needed was a ladder so we could reach them to put up the lovingly sewn curtains. Off we went to Lectoure to an electrical goods store recommended by Marie. We bought a vacuum cleaner and a refrigerator which were to be delivered that afternoon, then bought a large aluminium ladder which had to be transported sticking out through the sunroof. This reminded me of the time a few years earlier when Phillip and I bought a large Christmas tree and could not fit it into the boot of the car. We did not have a roof rack and were at our wits' end until Phillip came up with a clever (probably highly illegal) solution. I was to drive the car home slowly and he would partially lean out of his window holding the offending tree outside the car. We got many curious glances on the way home and were relieved not to have caused any accidents with all the heads turning around to see this strange sight. Fortunately the ladder did fit in through the roof rack and stuck straight up into the air with me inside, holding on like grim death.

That afternoon while the refrigerator was being delivered, Dominique and her little cousin, Marie-Pierre, rode into the courtyard on a spluttering scooter to deliver an invitation to dinner at her parents' house. We had been so busy getting rid of the squatters and rushing off to the shops that we had not yet gone across to say hello. Usually we stopped off at a super-market in Astaffort to buy essentials like cheese, bread, sausages and milk for our first night's meal in Larroque, but having arrived at midnight we had nothing to eat or drink in the house. We even needed gas for our little camping stove. Phillip cannot function without his two cups of very strong coffee first thing in the morning so grocery shopping was essential.

We saw deer in the woods near our village on several occa-sions but they were never close enough for us to photograph. Rabbits and cats frequently ran across the road when we were driving along while large dogs lay panting in front of their homes gazing at us with disinterest. The little pet poodles with their perfect coiffures were another matter. Even when being held tenderly under their mistresses' arms (we have yet to see *un homme* carrying one of these little dogs, usually called Fifi), they would yap as we passed by. Every time we have stopped at a petrol station on the *autoroute*, there have been people letting their dogs out for what needs to be done.

Dinner, as always, was a tremendous success. On this occasion another of Marie's cousins, Marc and his wife Jacqueline, their two little girls and pet dog were staying for their summer holiday. Marc worked for EDF and his wife was a teacher. We mentioned our squatters and Pierre said that we had had a wasps' nest in the attic the previous week and he had called the equivalent of the village pest control team to eradicate them. We were also told what to get for the little nest in the mailbox. I tasted *foie gras* for the first time and must confess I did not like it, mostly because of its greasy texture. The vivid descriptions we were given of the geese having funnels stuck down their throats, maize forced in and their necks massaged made me feel quite ill although we were assured the geese did not mind at all. Marie offered to take us to a neighbour who reared geese for this very purpose but we made some feeble excuse about having to put curtains up the next day. We were told to get on with our meal as we were going to a town about 20 kilometres away to *le marché de nuit* – a market which was open only during the night.

After dinner we followed Pierre's car as he shot down the narrow winding lanes at a surprising speed for a man who was usually slow and deliberate in his actions. Marc and family followed us. We had to park outside the town as all the roads were cordoned off to non-residents and walked through to the marketplace. There were hundreds of stalls selling all manner of goods, from hot food to numerous varieties of *pâté* and *foie gras*, strings of onions and plump garlic bulbs, olives of every size and hue, several varieties of dried sausage, handcrafted items, jewellery and shoes. Every few yards there were makeshift bars with tables and chairs and wine flowed freely. Loud music accompanied the proceedings and at the end of the town youngsters were dancing happily. We excused ourselves after an hour or so and tried to find our way home in the pitch dark, ending up in a town 50 kilometres away. Fortunately it had signs pointing to towns we were familiar with and we managed to get home by 1am.

We met the other wildlife on our estate when sitting outside one morning reading the novels we had brought with us. A little green lizard ventured out of a hole in the outside wall and leapt onto the new wall (which had the intact old tiles rescued from the hall and kitchen laid on top) and lay sunning himself.

Phillip photographing one our of our visitors – a lizard.

One of his family then decided to sneak into the house but was soon shooed outside again. We then noticed a little tabby kitten sitting high up on one of Pierre's haybales in our barn. It was too timid to come down and be fed but the Boivins later assured us it would survive on all the mice that were around. We were not to get it used to our food or it would starve when we left.

We were sorry that we could not bring Snowy, our little Siamese cat, and our dog, Shandy, with us because of the very strict British quarantine laws. We would have had to dump them on the Boivins and they had enough mouths to feed.

During our evening alfresco meal we were plagued by wasps who wanted our melons. Phillip hit on the idea of leaving an eaten half melon on the ground beside the table and this seemed to do the trick, for a short while at least. The wasps were very territorial about their own areas. They would fly around angrily whenever I tried to pick the lovely juicy black-berries that grew in abundance.

The next weekend was our village *fête* once again. This time our village lads (and a few grandfathers) won the tug of war though the greasy pole prize went once again to the valiant firefighters of our neighbouring village. Dominique was grow-ing up into a very pretty young lady with long dark hair and flashing brown eyes and had no shortage of dancing partners. She kept coming back to our table and dragging Phillip and me onto the dance floor to join in. Our octogenarian friend was there again, dancing merrily. We renewed old acquaintances and made new friends, including the owners of the Alsatian pup. They chain him up during the day but let him loose at night to patrol the grounds. Fortunately he regards us as friends now and comes leaping out of the bushes to welcome us whenever we have been away for long periods.

We rang home frequently but the telephone was always engaged. I finally had to ring a friend at work and ask her to telephone the children and ask them to stay off the phone for a couple of hours on Sunday so that I could tell them where the next week's money for groceries was hidden. I had no trouble getting through after that! Kathryn said they had searched everywhere for the hidden treasure but were unable to find it. The third week's money was even more carefully hidden and it was not until several months later that the children admitted they were pleased we had played this little game as it would have been easy to spend the whole lot at once. The girls told us that Snowy had developed a liking for Shandy's large bed and would stalk into it haughtily even if Shandy was lying in it. He would then leap out, treating the senior, though much smaller, member of the family with great deference and would squeeze himself into her little bed. They made such a funny picture!

Snowy the cat sitting comfortably in Shandy's bed while he squeezes into hers, sitting bolt upright.

It was wonderful having a fridge at last. We were able to have cold drinks and to store food without worrying about it going off. Grocery shopping in France was always fun. There was a glut of fresh fruit in summer – apricots, peaches, nectarines, pears and bananas, also several varieties of apples and plums. My favourite fruits were the greengages and I was quite happy to munch on these and *baguettes* with Boursin herb cheese for lunch while Phillip enjoyed his ham and mortadella. We were unsure of the different cuts of meat at the *boucherie* and stuck to lamb chops, the different varieties of sausage and the wonderful, lean, freshly ground minced beef (*hachée*) . Besides, we still did not have a cooker apart from the gas camping stove and a small two-ring electric table-top cooker. We discovered the packets of diced bacon *(lardons)* which were easy to use. The large white onions had a sweet, delicate flavour and tomato and onion salad became a daily favourite.

On Wednesdays our local town held its outdoor *marché*, while the covered market was open on Thursdays and Saturdays. The covered market had some large stalls with overflowing baskets of fresh produce right by the entrance. Further along there were small tables mostly manned by an elderly man or woman, offering perhaps a basket of eggs or a small collection of home-grown tomatoes. Several had plaits of garlic, some tied with pretty ribbon. These made super gifts for friends back home. I always felt we should help these older folk and tended to buy at least one of the items we needed from them. There were other stalls selling *foie gras, pâté de foie gras, confit de canard* (potted duck) and lots of varieties of fresh and dried sausages. There were also cheeses of various types. At one end was a little bar where coffee and soft drinks were available.

Outside, on either side of the entrance were plants and

flowers for sale. I longed for the day when we could have flowering plants on our terrace at Larroque but that would have to wait until we lived there. I did foolishly plant a hibiscus in the *jardinière* and a bougainvillaea near the rose bushes but both were dead the next time we were back in Larroque.

The Wednesday market meant parking became difficult unless

A stallholder at our local market.

we arrived very early because the centre of the town was now filled with market stalls and vans selling a huge variety of goods. There were stalls selling beautiful, bright Provençal fabrics for curtains, tablecloths and napkins, the readymade items were also available. Material tended to be more expensive in France we noticed. Nevertheless I bought some bright yellow Provençal fabric with the typical blue print to make a tablecloth for the small kitchen table. There were dresses, skirts, blouses, menswear and childrenswear stalls, household goods and gardening tools. We just could not resist a large glazed yellow pottery fruit bowl as it would look perfect in our new kitchen. We then had to buy a second one for a friend back home. The stallholder was from another region and, unfortunately, we never saw him again or Larroque would be filled with pretty glazed pottery.

We had bravely invited the Boivins, Janet, Marc and family for dinner warning them that we did not have a proper cooker as yet. Larroque was a hive of activity that day. We decided on a colourful starter arranging slices of hard-boiled egg around a pile of cherry tomatoes, next a ring of avocado slices, finally tomato slices, drizzled with olive oil and finished with sprinkled capers. We had made sure there was enough *'ping'* to keep everyone happy. For the main course I decided on meat balls in a special sauce *à la Grace* as they could be cooked in batches in the Sunbeam electric multicooker. These were accompanied by green beans and sautéed potatoes. I added fried onions to the potatoes for a bit of fun. We had discovered a cheese we had not tasted before – *Cantal* – which was full of flavour, also a *fromage d'Auvergne* and had English crackers as an accompaniment. Dessert was fresh fruit salad with a *soupçon* of Armagnac, served with ice cream. As our dining table only seated six we placed it end to end with the outdoor plastic table, covering each with a matching new flower-printed bedsheet bought for that very purpose at our local market. We had fragrant roses from our own garden decorating the tables, the new crocheted lace door curtain and all the window curtains were up making the house inviting.

Our guests came laden with gifts, not only fresh produce but also a large *tarte de Gascogne* and a housewarming present – a lovely copper plate depicting a family scene (from Marc and his family whom we had known for only a few days). They did justice to the meal and were persuaded to try the sloe gin we had made the previous year – it met with universal approval. Marc suddenly jumped up and dashed out. Pierre assured us he was all right and he was soon back brandishing his guitar. We had a wonderful time singing French and English songs well into the night.

Roads in the French countryside can be rather daunting not only because they are narrow but they also have deep ditches on either side. Yet it seems to be a matter of pride not to slow down at all even in the face of rapidly advancing oncoming traffic. We had an interesting encounter with just such a ditch. After visiting the Boivins one afternoon we got into our car to drive back to Larroque. We could not drive around their home as there were several cars belonging to sundry visitors blocking our way. Phillip decided to reverse onto the road and did so in his usual energetic manner. A second later our car was partly in the ditch at the side of the road and there was no way Phillip could get it out. Pierre had been watching us leave and saw what happened. He rushed to his tractor and chugged slowly towards us, attached a tow rope to the front of our car and yanked us out of the ditch neatly and quickly. We thanked Pierre effusively and sheepishly drove home keeping to the centre of the road.

The night before leaving Larroque we moved all the furniture back into the second front room which was mouse-proof, packed the car and covered all the kitchen work surfaces and the tables with newspaper to keep off as much dust as possible. This was inevitable while there was still work to be done on the house.

Chapter Nine

Of this and that

There were two routes we could take from our village to our local town, both more or less the same distance. One road led from our village through the immaculate little village nearby with about eight 'sleeping policemen' and orderly rows of alternating trees with red leaves and green leaves. There was a tiny village square or *place* opposite the trim *Mairie* where their annual *fête* was held. The homeowners took great pride in their gardens and had palm trees, banana plants (we never saw any bananas on them), and beautiful trumpet vines, some climbers, others that were growing upright like trees, all with gorgeous orange to red flowers.

The old lady who lived in one of the houses often stood by her gate surrounded by colourful petunias, watching the world go by. Some days we would see her watering her collection of plants, many of them growing in old tins, jugs, basins and drums as well as in conventional pots. One house had an arbour which supported grapevines bearing heavy bunches of glistening grapes. There were some houses that had terraces, others which had small shady gardens in front of them, but they all had a little table and chairs for outside dining. The French people always sat in the shade, however, unlike a certain Irishman I know.

One day while driving through this little village we noticed a new sign on a house at the end of a row, next to the *Mairie*, which read *'Café du Sport'*. Two tiny tables each with a chair on either side now sat invitingly on the little terrace in front of the café. We just had to stop not only for a drink, also because I wanted to have a closer look at the tiny stone house opposite

The Café du Sport

which had a cardboard sign hanging from the door knob, '*A
Vendre*' – For Sale. It looked like a one-up, one-down cottage
but it did have a walled garden – another of my fantasies. The
door and shutters were rotten and the rooms looked dark and
small from the outside. A few years later while driving through
we noticed that the For Sale sign had been removed, the tiny
house had been freshly painted and had a new door and windows. It looked cared for and we were pleased that it now had
a new owner. We ordered our Cokes *(Coka)* and were enjoying

sitting outside when the bartender, possibly also the owner, came out and asked Phillip *"Vous êtes acteur?"* adding that he had seen him on television and in the cinema. We were totally bemused, not sure we had understood correctly, but he repeated himself and said Phillip was Philippe Noiret, a famous French actor. Phillip confessed he was not and the man insisted that he looked exactly like his famous counterpart. As we drove off Phillip smoothed his beard and patted down his hair, looking quite smug because he resembled a famous actor. I felt mildly peeved because I had been totally ignored, obviously not having even a passing resemblance to anyone who mattered. For days we wondered what the actor looked like, as even Marie and Pierre could see a resemblance. Then one day when we were out with the Boivins we saw a poster advertising a film starring Philippe Noiret. He looked ancient with his white beard and Dominique laughed as she pointed him out to Phillip, saying there was his double. We are no longer allowed to mention certain French actors in our house! I personally think that Phillip resembles Sean Connery – who needs a French actor?

The other road from our village to our town takes us through yet another small village consisting of a handful of houses built around a small chateau. It does have a petrol pump on the pavement, one small grocery *(épicerie)* and the *boulangerie* owned by our friend *Monsieur le Boulanger*. There is a small café at one end of the village, at the other end is a beautiful hotel which is being renovated by an English couple in the traditional Gascogne style. We have not visited it as yet. The villagers enjoy sitting outside their front doors (which open onto the pavement) and having a good chat or just watching the world go by. The chateau, though small, has a gorgeous garden, partly walled, with lots of palm trees, bougainvillaea, hibiscus and pomegranate bushes. Virginia creeper drapes the garden walls. The courtyard is paved, exactly what I would like to do at Larroque should I somehow accumulate a fortune.

One of our favourite places to visit is a little fortified village (*un bastide*)about 25 kilometres away. It is built in the form of a circle and many of the houses have Virginia creeper spilling along the walls with petunias and Busy Lizzies vying for space on the terraces. Ancient oak beams hold up the covered arches and the paving stones are worn smooth with centuries of use. The central area is circular with plane trees providing shade for the *pétanque* players and their fans. There is a small chateau at one end, two little restaurants and a small museum within the *bastide* itself. On the outside of the village there runs a little river and the houses facing the outside have flower-bedecked terraces overlooking the river with its beautiful views. We have sometimes thought it would be lovely to live in one of these houses but we would miss being near the Boivins. There is a small church the other side of the river. No matter how small the French village it always seems to have at least one church and a monument to the soldiers who died for their country.

Our village has had its share of tragedy. One summer we were told by a tearful Marie that four teenagers were killed when their car crashed into the only tree on the narrow road between our village and that of *Monsieur le Boulanger*. The youngsters had not been drinking, they had gone out for a drive and were possibly driving too fast on the hairpin bends that make up much of this road.

Phillip and I had a miraculous escape in what could have been a very nasty accident. Instead of leaving Larroque at 3am as planned to catch the noon ferry, we left at 8pm, as Phillip was adamant that he could stay awake and drive through the night. He had lots of strong coffee before we left, we had a

Thermos flask with more coffee in the car and we made a few stops for petrol and more coffee. There was no way I could keep awake and dozed off only to be rudely awakened by the car ramming itself against the central metal barrier on the *autoroute*, then against the barrier on the right with Phillip valiantly trying to control the steering wheel. This happened a few times then the car swerved across a gap in the central barrier, across the lanes on the other side, onto a side road and bounced into a ditch where it finally stopped. Miraculously we did not suffer even a scratch. The front of the car was crumpled in, as was the boot. Fortunately there were no other cars on the road while the drama took place although it was about 6am. A kind farmer hauled us out of the ditch with his tractor and would not accept any payment for his trouble. There were bits of metal preventing one of the front wheels from turning and Phillip had to forcibly straighten the metal fragments before we could slowly drive on to Cherbourg. The soundtrack of *Flashdance* was blaring loudly during the accident and I have not been able to listen to it since although it was one of my favourite CDs. We were also extremely lucky to have enough petrol to limp home as the petrol cap had been rammed in and could not be opened. We think the BMW is a wonderful car – it saved our lives. Even the eggs in the food hamper in the back of the car were intact!

Another sad event occurred just before the summer *fête*. A young carpenter who lived in our village was working at home, installing what sounded like a very large wardrobe with mirrored doors. From what we understood the wardrobe fell on him, the mirrors broke and fatally injured him. What a shock for his wife to discover when she returned home! The *fête* was cancelled that year as a mark of respect.

One day we were telling the Boivins about our discovery – a

store which stocked beautiful solid furniture, saying that one day we would like a buy a huge oak table for our massive dining room when Pierre leapt up saying, *"On y va"* and ushered us into his car. We drove down one of the many narrow winding roads leading out of our village and entered a farmyard which was part carpenter shop. There were huge piles of timber neatly stacked according to size. We were introduced to *Monsieur le Charpentier* who, after some crossfire in *'ping'* accents, invited us into his home. We were offered *apéritifs* and then, proudly, the covers (there were at least four) were pulled off the kitchen table to expose a gleaming solid oak dining table. That was not all. We were then shown into the sitting room where an even grander table was uncovered, this one of cherry wood. The craftsmanship was exquisite down to the beautifully carved legs. I now began to lust seriously after a table such as this, even the Aga was forgotten in this sudden rush of infatuation. When we asked timidly what it would cost we were told about 9000 French francs – about £1000 – nothing like the price we would expect to pay for such a piece back home. He did add however, that he was so busy with orders that it would be at least a year before he could even think of making us a table. As time passed we realised that we had to spend a vast amount of money on necessary repairs and renovations such as new shutters and windows, and laying gravel down on our courtyard (it was the cheapest way of addressing the sticky mud and clay puddles that developed every time it rained) and we never did order the table.

Once the major renovations on the house had been completed we started thinking about the garden. My colleagues at work had given us some pretty shrubs which were thriving but I wanted shade so I could sit out on the *terrasse* with Phillip without blistering my skin. I asked Yves to plant one red-leafed and one green-leafed tree just beyond the terrace in front of the house. He brought his gardening catalogue along and we had fun choosing other trees. We decided on a wisteria to train against the wall of the stable as that was quite bare, a weeping willow to plant near the pond, a *Campsis radicans* (trumpet vine) to go near the rose bushes and four cedars of Lebanon to be positioned around the edge of the courtyard. Later on I wanted a low wall built around the upper level and wide steps going down to the lower level where the chicken house and Grace's version of Monet's garden would be. The chicken house was to be spruced up and painted like Monet's house and certainly would not accommodate chickens. They would have to live in one of the other outbuildings. For obvious reasons the landscaping would only be done when we were living permanently in France. At that time I would also have an arbour built over the terrace along the south-facing wall and train grapevines up the wooden posts. *Voilà*! I would then have more shade and fresh grapes to nibble on while indulging in my other passions – painting and tapestry.

The trees flourished from the first year that they were planted and grew slowly but surely. Pierre rigged up a makeshift garden hose by connecting together several bits of hose and wrapping the joints in plastic, watering the little trees on really hot days when we were not in residence. The third summer the two trees were about five feet tall. The cedars of Lebanon grew much more slowly, as we had anticipated. However, there was also a dense growth of weeds all over our beautiful gravel courtyard. Phillip had splashed out on a brand new petrol strimmer before we left England and spent much of his time striding about our land brandishing the strimmer and producing some semblance of a lawn where there once was tall hay and undergrowth. He would come back from his forays soaking wet with all his exertion, his chest and back mahogany brown and his legs covered with long scratches and gashes from flying stones and debris. It was too hot to wear trousers but shorts just did not provide enough protection. My pleas to strim in the cool of the day, wearing long trousers, fell on deaf ears because part of the fun for him was being out in the blistering sun! We certainly got through a lot of lemonade and Coca-Cola that summer. After the long grass, his next attack was on the weeds growing through the gravel. Phillip bought the most potent weedkiller he could find, probably sent to Iraq for it, used my new watering can to mix the solution and then strode through the courtyard carefully measuring out the dose. It worked! On our next trip to Larroque a few months later the weeds were sad little brown heaps but my little green-leafed tree was also a casualty. I was terribly upset. Obviously the weedkiller had got too near that tree. Desperate life-saving measures were called for. I pruned off the dead top of the tree and trained a little live side shoot up along the stake. Now, three years later, the tree looks normal through not as tall as the red one. Weedkillers are now *interdit* near my plants. I had to buy a third watering can and hide it as my beloved husband would use whatever he could find to mix the weedkiller in and then could never remember whether it was contaminated or not! I think the only thing I have managed to wean him off is depositing cigarette ash in the saucer of his coffee cup, persuading him to use an ashtray instead. Even this does not always work.

Yves, in between renovating bits of Larroque for us, was building swimming pools for other homeowners in the area, apparently a lucrative occupation. When I had got to the stage that I could not reach the rendering on the front of the house even with our ladder, we asked Yves to do the job for us. He transformed the front of Larroque, both the house and the stable (which originally showed the breeze block and bricks from which it was constructed). He also tidied up the back of the house getting rid of the cages and wire netting, strengthening the roof and tiling the roof of the bread oven. Now the only problem was that the poor wisteria gave up the struggle for life after being smothered in plaster, cement and other building materials. One day we will plant another one. Meanwhile the cedars of Lebanon are growing slowly and are now almost my height.

We were awakened one summer morning at about 8am by the sound of drilling and heavy machinery, seemingly just outside our bedroom window. I rushed out to find a huge machine with a crane lifting and depositing a large concrete post at the side of our open haybarn, next to the old wooden post which supported the electricity cables. A vague memory of correspondence from EDF *(Electricité de France)* about replacing the old posts sprang to mind. The work was completed in a few minutes and the men then drove their monster truck around the back of the house and down the side to replace the post there. We now have three new concrete electricity posts on our property.

One spring we took advantage of a *Sunday Times* offer of a weekend in Giverny with tickets to Monet's garden and the opportunity to stay in a chateau near the gardens. The price was very reasonable and we lost no time booking our first available weekend. It was April, the sun was shining in France and we drove along with the top of Phillip's Lotus Elan down and the wind blowing through our hair. We arrived at the chateau which was very elegant and had beautiful views overlooking the river. However, the free bottle of wine did not make up for our disappointment on learning that there were no vacant rooms in the chateau but that we would be staying in the annexe across the road. This was probably the servants' quarters in days of yore and had no view whatsoever apart from the chateau car park in front and a high wall at the back. Our room was small and the walls appeared to be covered in copper – it was probably just metallic wallpaper. The bathroom was small and the floor got soaking wet every time we used the shower, as did our clothes and all the towels. We had to enlist each other's help to bring in a dry towel when we turned the shower off. There were compensations – the evening meal in the chateau dining room was delicious and we were much amused by the antics of one of the guests. He drank his way through several bottles of wine, complained loudly about the food and service (in English of course), much to the embarrassment of his wife who left halfway through the meal. The other English couple with them tried to reason with him but he just got more garrulous and then strode off into the bar where he continued to drink while propositioning every woman who happened to pass through.

Monet's house and gardens at Giverny more than made up for our disappointment with the accommodation. We decided to go early as we knew it would be crowded. Even so there were hordes of people there with more coachloads arriving every few minutes. There were long queues waiting to tour the house so we decided to wander around the gardens first. The roses were unbelievable – bunches of fragrant blooms seemed almost to weigh the bushes down. We ambled through the archways supporting clematis of several varieties and strolled along pathways lined by poppies of varying shades of pink and red. The river with the famous Japanese bridge was immediately recognisable but the wisteria was not yet in bloom. The waterlilies appeared to be flourishing and there were masses of other flowering bushes lining the banks of the river. Later on in the morning when we wandered back to the Japanese bridge we saw a bride and groom posing on it for photographs. The back view of the bridal dress, which was all we could see of the bride, was fabulous. It had exquisite cutwork embroidery from the neckline to the waist and suited the slender bride perfectly. The groom happened to turn around and saw us so we waved and he then asked his bride to turn around so we could see her. She was beautiful and obviously ecstatically happy. The front of the dress was simplicity itself in contrast to the elaborate embroidery on the back, but stunning. The wedding photographs in that setting must have been memorable. Our tour around the house was not particularly enjoyable because of the ever-increasing crowds. We could not fully appreciate the pictures and décor of the various rooms so went back to enjoy the garden.

Phillip was busy photographing the gorgeous flowers, as that is one of his hobbies. I wandered along trying to improve my French by eavesdropping on conversations. Many of the visitors, however, were British. I suddenly realised that a man passing by was gesticulating at me saying,"*Madame, votre robe!*" For one awful moment I thought something horrible had happened to the dress I was wearing, a long turquoise blue, floaty one with buttons all the way down the front, then realised he was pointing to a large wasp on the skirt. I quickly brushed it off, thanking him with heartfelt gratitude. I had had two previous nasty encounters with wasps. Once, when I was about ten I went camping with our Girl Guides troop. We discovered an old boat sitting at the side of a river and promptly climbed into it. I unluckily grasped the wooden seat before sitting down and was stung with vigour. It was most unpleasant. Then, recently, we were sitting down to lunch at the Boivins when I leaned back on my seat and was stung on my back. I bravely stifled a scream and told Phillip that I had been stung by a wasp.

In typically male fashion he said, "You couldn't have been! If it was a wasp you would have known it!" assuming that I had not felt enough pain because I did not shout and yell. I think that women certainly make much less fuss than men and also tolerate pain better.

The little gift shop within the Giverny gardens had beautiful but somewhat expensive items for sale so we went to the shop outside, in the car park nearby. This had packets of seeds in addition to the usual souvenirs so I bought a few packets and did not realise until I was outside the shop that I had been grossly overcharged by the sullen girl at the till. *C'est la vie!* As we had entry tickets for two days we returned on Sunday to bask in the sunshine and watch the flowers grow until it was time to leave for the drive back to the ferry.

Chapter Ten

Interludes in Spain

One autumn while we were at Larroque, Dominique came across to ask whether we would like to accompany Pierre, François, herself and Claude on a trip to Spain. *"Bien sur"* (of course) we said, not wanting to miss out on any fun. Marie could not go as she had hundreds of tiny quail chicks to feed. We had seen her 'foster children' a few days before. They were darling little birds, cheeky and unafraid, ready to dash outside the moment the door to the huge barn was opened. In another shed Marie had hundreds of chicks which were just the opposite. When the door was opened they all rushed to the centre of the barn and huddled together in a panic. Poor Marie had to stay home and babysit. We asked who Claude was and were told he was Dominique's *copain* or *petit ami* (boyfriend). Claude was a handsome young man who was obviously besotted with our Dominique. He worked in a local *charcuterie* and was responsible for preparing and canning the *foie gras*.

Claude drove the Boivins at high speed and we followed gamely, enjoying the beautiful day. The route was spectacular with the Pyrenees in the distance at first and then, in no time at all we were driving around the foothills and past the border into Spain. The houses started to look different from those of Gascony as we approached the Pyrenees. They were now mostly grey in colour and made of smaller stones, not the large pale golden stones of our area. The road ran alongside a fairly large, rapidly moving river, winding through picturesque scenery, much of it hilly. Further along was a small town where we stopped to look at the shops before lunch. There were many handmade items, lace, clothing, pottery and little purses made of the softest leather. I could not resist buying a couple for Kathryn and Sharon, one a tiny rucksack and the other a small pouch with a leather drawstring. Steve got a multipurpose penknife. I was pleased to be able to sample a Spanish *tortilla* – a sort of fairly solid omelette with potatoes and onions. My mouth waters just thinking about it, I must try and find a recipe. That was accompanied by lovely fresh bread. I believe Phillip had steak yet again as did the others, accompanied by piles of *pommes frites* (chips). We left the restaurant to find that it was pouring with rain and the river was now a torrent, churning and foaming as it rushed along. We dashed to our cars and followed Claude to another town on the outskirts of which was a huge supermarket. This made the huge *super-marchés* at the ferry ports look insignificant. There were all kinds of meats, cheeses, wines and spirits, household items and toys. I was tempted by a Spanish sweet in the form of a roll made with pinenuts and honey. We bought a couple of bottles of wine and watched with some interest as Pierre and François loaded two trolleys with bottles of wine and beer and then proceeded to fill a third one. Apparently they stocked up here once a year as alcohol was much cheaper here than in France. Fortunately we had enough space in our car for much of their shopping.

We got home somewhat damp but soon dried out in front of our gas heater with its huge gas cylinder. In winter this was a great boon as it quickly heated up the large rooms and was movable. We tended to sit in the kitchen in the evenings, in front of the gas fire, reading and listening to our favourite CDs. Before we bought the gas heater all we had was a little electric fire. Phillip and I used to sit huddled up in our garden chairs as close as we dared to the fire. Our feet used to get really hot while the rest of us stayed cold. We have always been reluctant to light fires in the newly renovated fireplaces even though the chimneys have been swept. We opted against one of the monstrous white gas cylinders that sit in the garden as they are certainly not pretty and Yves would have to drill holes in the stone walls to connect the pipes.

The day after our trip to Spain we heard from Pierre that the torrential rain had caused severe flooding in the area we had visited and a nearby campsite was washed away that night with several fatalities. What a disastrous end to a lovely camping holiday!

My next visit to Spain was in May to attend an international scientific conference which was being held in Madrid. My colleague, Barbara (who had accompanied me on the curtain-shopping spree in Houston) and I tried our best to fit in a few days at Larroque but this was not possible as we had to attend the sessions every day. We worked until 4pm on the day of our departure and then drove as fast as it was possible during the rush hour to the airport long term car park, realising we had not given ourselves enough time. We leapt off the shuttle bus from the car park at the wrong terminal and then had to find our way back to the correct one. In the meantime the minutes were ticking past and we arrived at the check-in desk to find all the seats had been allocated and there was no room for us. (To this day I cannot understand why airlines double book several seats!). There were no other flights that day and we would be missing most of the next day's conference so we felt pretty miserable, but were then told we were being upgraded to Club class. We accepted graciously and thoroughly enjoyed the rest of the trip.

The hotel was a very up-market one in the centre of Madrid, absolutely packed out with delegates to our conference, including several hundred Japanese and their spouses. It was quite late when we strolled out of the hotel looking for a restaurant nearby for dinner. After a delicious meal accompanied by sangria we stopped in a bar on the way home for a nightcap and found to our delight that this was accompanied by a large bowl of salted almonds. On the way back to the hotel we saw several young girls who seemed to be in their early teens, dressed in incredibly short skirts and very high-heeled boots plying their trade along the street, even in front of the hotel. This seemed to be quite acceptable although it came as a shock to Barbara and myself as we both had daughters older than the youngsters on the streets. Police cars also drove by but no one interfered with the goings on. It seemed rather strange to us that this was allowed in the more affluent areas of Madrid. After the morning session the next day we walked into Madrid to explore the city and do some shopping. We accidentally bumped into a middle-aged Spanish couple who stopped when they heard our "Oops! Sorry!" and asked us whether we were on our own and why did we not have an escort in such a dangerous city. Their English was not perfect, our Spanish was non-existent but we managed to keep a conversation going. The lady then gave her plastic bags of shopping to her husband, took each of us by the arm and said they would accompany us to the shopping area because there were many thieves around. Our first stop at their insistence was at a *tapas* bar. This was a very large room with a bar in the centre and with large cured hams hanging from the ceiling, jostling for space just like the customers on the floor. We were offered some red wine and plates heaped with paper-thin slices of ham carved off one of those that were hanging up. We were told there were several different varieties and that we could stay there all afternoon tasting them. All things considered, we felt it would be prudent to move on before too much wine was pressed upon us. Every few minutes the wife checked to make sure we still had our handbags and they even escorted us into the various stores. Eventually we decided to forget about shopping and invited them to have coffee with us before they went back to their daughter's home (they were visiting from a small village some distance away). The café was another unique experience – the coffee was served in glasses, but still delicious and with it we had strange coils of what looked like fried pastry. We were also given melted chocolate in which to dip the sausage-like strips. On the whole I think I prefer the savoury Spanish *tortilla* made with potatoes and eggs, a sort of cross between an omelette and a flan.

Although Barbara and I got back to the hotel safely, thinking the couple had exaggerated somewhat about the dangers of Madrid, we soon found out that they were absolutely right. That evening the British conference delegates were invited to a reception at the British Consulate headquarters – a fabulous house with a beautiful garden. We heard there that one of the ladies had gone out with her sister and had been mugged with her handbag stolen, right in the middle of the street. We made sure we stayed in large groups after hearing about that incident.

The Conference reception was held in another large hotel quite a distance away so we were transported there in several coaches. The huge hall had numerous tables groaning under the weight of all kinds of delicious food ranging from cold meats, vegetables, salads and dips to gorgeous desserts and a vast array of fruit. The British delegates queued up politely and started helping themselves to modest amounts of savoury foods. Just then the Japanese delegates arrived and pushed past us to the tables, grabbed plates and heaped piles of food on, mixing together sweet and savoury dishes and fruit. In a few minutes all the serving dishes were empty and we polite, restrained Brits waited patiently for refills to appear. This crowd behaviour was totally the opposite of what Barbara and I had experienced on a previous visit to Tokyo for a conference. The people on the streets were extremely courteous, bowed when they spoke (in Japanese, of course) and were very careful not to brush against anyone. At the formal Conference dinner we were amazed by the military precision with which the army of waiters and waitresses served and removed each course (whether or not one had finished it by the time the Head Waiter gave his nod). The other impression we came away with was how expensive everything was in Tokyo – the hotels, the clothes, the food and even the coffee (the equivalent of £5.00 a cup).

Back in Madrid the other memorable event was a Flamenco ballet to which we were invited as part of the social activities of the conference. The dancing was superb, full of passion and fire, quite unlike any other ballets we had seen. On our way back to the airport we drove past fields of asparagus and beautiful Mediterranean-style houses with lovely archways thickly covered with bougainvillaea. Pretty as they were they did not have the appeal of Larroque and there was no temptation to even enquire how much they cost. This, of course, was music to Phillip's ears.

Although not really Spanish, a typical family outing in the South-West of France is to the much-feted *corrida*, a sort of Portuguese bull-fight. Dominique arrived one afternoon to tell us we were expected for dinner that evening at her parents' home but it would have to be early as we were going with them to *la corrida*. I was not particularly keen but we felt it would be churlish to eat and then leave so we all set off to the town where the festivities were held each year. As usual we had to park outside the town under the watchful eyes of the local *gendarmerie* and walk to the arena. The place was packed with families, all of whom had brought children of various ages, from about two upwards. We sat on tiered benches not quite sure what to expect. The evening started with a line of ten young boys all dressed up in satin finery, with hats on, walking in to loud cheering. A fairly benign-looking bull was then let into the enclosure and the first young lad ran up to it, grabbed it by the horns and tried to wrestle it to the ground. Naturally the bull was having none of this and tossed the boy to the ground. The second lad in line then attempted a similar feat with the bull and got the same treatment. This went on until all the boys had been thrown down and had their clothes ripped, some even had blood drawn, but they then strode off proudly to much applause while an older bullfighter managed to get the bull out of the ring. Now the real 'sport' began. Each bull was let into the ring and taunted by two or three bullfighters, all in splendid regalia, first whisking capes in front of it then throwing long thin spears at it. The spears stuck in the bull's back and sides with blood dripping down. The taunting continued with the bull becoming more and more enraged, charging wildly until it was tired and weak with loss of blood. One final bullfighter then wrestled with the bull and it was dragged down. I spent most of the evening covering my eyes, much to the astonishment of the children nearby who were obviously used to it and not perturbed by the events. The most upsetting bit of all was when one of the bulls just stood placidly in the ring, gazing at the crowds with large brown eyes, not realising what was happening to him. He just kept turning around each time a spear was thrown at him, looking more and more bewildered. We made our excuses and left feeling profoundly grateful that we were not born bulls.

The next summer we were invited to spend a weekend with friends who lived in Barcelona. Trini is a doctor who had spent some time training in London so we had got to know her quite well and had also met José, her husband. We planned our route from Larroque carefully using one of the passes through the Pyrenees rather than taking the *autoroute* all the way along the coast. We left fairly early on the Friday morning but got stuck in horrendous traffic for hours. Fortunately we had some food and soft drinks (rather warm) in the car so did not mind sitting stationary apart from the blazing sun. We finally arrived at 8.30pm at our appointed meeting place – a large department store, El Corte Inglés. We followed José and Trini through streets full of cars, all honking vigorously for no apparent reason. Air-conditioning in cars was imperative during the Barcelona summer as the heat was unbearable. We noticed a small irritating habit that most of the drivers seemed to have – they would never use their hand brakes when they stopped at traffic lights. Consequently whenever the lights changed, all the lines of cars would slide back then move forward. I suppose enough space was left between cars to cater for this habit and prevent damage when sliding back! Perhaps the cars in Spain do not have hand brakes!!

We stayed with Trini and José in a beautiful apartment in the centre of Barcelona. Just after midnight we were told it was Spanish dinner time and we sallied forth to the waterfront where there were seafood restaurants galore. Phillip is a great seafood fan while I prefer not to even have to look at, let alone eat, strange creatures with shells and goodness knows how many legs. The restaurants had tanks of live fish and other sea creatures from which the customer could choose his dinner and have it cooked to his taste. Grilled sardines were my choice while Phillip was urged to try the 'Seafood Special". While we waited for the food to arrive (an hour later) we had lovely fresh warm bread spread with fresh tomato pulp and with a drizzle of olive oil added – delicious! Our food then arrived, normal sized plates for three of us but a huge bowl for Phillip, filled with all manner of shells, pincers, legs and evil-eyed creatures which appeared to be staring at him. He was horrified to have to resort to DIY (do-it-yourself) to get his meal out of the shells, pincers and claws, using the tools that were handed to him. I don't know what he found worse, my gasp of horror or Trini and José beaming happily because he had the meal they thought he would enjoy.

The night was unbearably hot and sticky. Even having the fan on full blast did not ease the discomfort and I woke up in the middle of the night to find that Phillip had disappeared from the bedroom. He was lying on a towel on the small balcony practically gasping for air; he gets very uncomfortable in high humidity. We did enjoy Barcelona the next day in spite of the unrelenting heat. The Gaudí public park with its intriguing mosaics and the Church of the *Sagrada Familia* were fascinating to wander through. For the inner man there were several *'tapas'* bars that we visited, testing their delicacies and wines. The second evening was another culinary shock. We had dinner at a typical Catalonian restaurant (again after midnight). The room we entered looked like a butcher's shop with glass topped counters and shelves of raw meat. A door opened into the restaurant proper which was artistically decorated with pottery and vividly coloured paintings. The menu was either steak, the smallest serving being 14 ounces, or baby lamb so I chose the latter, Phillip the former, naturally. My starter was a tasty plateful of grilled aubergines and sweet peppers with plenty of fresh bread. The main courses then arrived. Phillip's steak was spilling over his plate and as for mine – it was literally half a baby lamb sliced down its middle and grilled, all 18 inches of it on a large plate. I felt quite ill looking at all the ribs and the neatly sectioned backbone. It was too young to have much meat on it or perhaps it had been malnourished. Phillip refused point blank to have any of my lamb so poor José offered to eat the offending dish.

After dinner we drove to one of the well-known tourist areas where we sipped coffee and watched a troupe of flamenco dancers twirling and stamping with remarkable grace and agility. The women managed to look haughty even while performing the most intricate steps. Then came the fireworks by the fountain, accompanied by classical music to suit. It was really late when we staggered back to the car to head home to bed.

Instead of driving back across the Pyrenees we decided to take the longer route and drive through Roussillon. The mountain scenery was exquisite with its forests and rivers but it was a bit too lonely for my taste. Phillip loved the area and hinted, in not too subtle a fashion, that we should perhaps consider buying a house in this region should we tire of Larroque. We stopped for an ice cream at a small restaurant high up in the hills and asked the owner whether many people passed that way. He managed to make a living in the summer but had to close the restaurant during the winter as it was in such an isolated location. I went to wash my hands after the delicious ice cream and then discovered to my horror that I was locked in the ladies' room. I tried for about five long minutes to open the door by turning the handle in every possible direction and then had to bang on the door to be let out. Most embarrassing!

We had enjoyed our weekend in Barcelona and were sorry to

leave our friends but were pleased to get back to Larroque with our cool shady house, early dinners and early to bed routine. We decided we must be getting old.

Chapter Eleven

Summer highlights

We did not have a telephone at Larroque and in the early days before we decided we were upwardly mobile enough to have cellular phones we were totally cut off from contact. Most times this was a good thing as Larroque was our escape from the usual pressures of work and domestic crises and we could only be contacted by letter. The small village a few kilometres to the east of us has a pay-phone in a little booth which we came to refer to as our phone as we never saw anyone else using it. The kiosk was always clean and never vandalised, the only signs of it having been used were the scores of cigarette butts strewn on the ground outside.

Once Larroque became habitable visitors started arriving. Our first house guests were Phillip's daughter (my stepdaughter) Andrea and her friend Nicola, both medical students at the time. They had arranged before we left England that they would arrive on Saturday, first flying to Bordeaux and then hiring bikes and riding to our village. However, we had absolutely no details about the times of the flights and were becoming concerned about the time it would take them to cycle over 100 kilometres so decided to phone for further information on Friday. The plans had been changed and the two youngsters were now travelling by train to Paris, spending some time there and then taking the train to Bordeaux so we would have to meet them there. The guest bedroom looked pretty with its pink curtains and little bowl of fragrant roses from the garden on the bedside table. We did not have any spare beds at that stage but the inflatable mattress was pumped up in readiness for the sleeping bags the girls were bringing. The new French towels purchased from our local market were neatly placed on the two chairs which constituted the only other furniture in the room.

We decided on a leisurely drive to Bordeaux avoiding the busy *autoroute* but got caught up in heavy traffic nevertheless. In addition to the usual cars and caravans we saw the strangest sight. A car was towing a small trailer consisting of a fairly large wooden tray on wheels on which a happy dog sat bolt upright, watching the world go by. We had to laugh but felt a twinge of guilt that Shandy would be unlikely to have such a treat as it would probably be illegal in England and there was no way we could bring him to France because of the strict quarantine laws on returning to the U.K. Snowy too would have loved running around the house and barn at Larroque.

It was good to see the girls who by that time were hungry and ready for whatever the Pizzeria had to offer. Andrea is a vegetarian and had no problems finding a suitable pizza. The *tiramisu* that we had for dessert was out of this world, oozing liqueur and topped with delicious cream.

A curious sight – a car towing a small trailer in which the family pet has a ride.

The next day the girls hired bicycles and set off to explore armed with sunscreen cream and bottles of water. In the afternoon the swimming pool in our local town proved irresistible. Meals cooked at home were a bit of a problem as Phillip eats only meat and thinks any food without legs such as lettuce or vegetables is meant for rabbits. My favourite breakfast (and sometimes dinner) muesli should be given to horses according to him as he much prefers bacon, eggs and sausages. He loves snails and *moules marinière* whereas I would far rather have a *croque-monsieur* – the French equivalent of Welsh rarebit. We discovered that the fridge and freezer were filled with meat of various sorts and there was not a lot that I could cook for poor Andrea the first day apart from potatoes. Fortunately she does eat eggs and cheese.

We had discovered riding stables in our town and decided to take Andrea and Nicola there one afternoon as they both loved riding. Phillip had never been on a horse but decided to give it a try while I opted for a quiet read and a bit of crochet in the cool house. When they returned Phillip had a rather dashing deep brown tan. Apparently he was given a huge, placid horse which ambled along the trail through fields of sunflowers in the blazing sun. He had worn shorts not realising that long trousers were essential garb for riding and had not worn a hat as he does not own one. It wasn't until he stiffly dismounted from the horse that he noticed that his legs seemed to be bowed outwards and, what was worse, he was severely chafed from not wearing the proper riding clothes. He did enjoy the ride although he could not sit down comfortably for several days thereafter. The only other time Phillip had ridden any sort of animal was in Karachi during a lecture tour. On one of our evenings off we were taken to the local beach where gaudily-bedecked camels were available for rides. Phillip bravely offered to accompany the small daughter of our hosts on a camel ride. The huge creature was persuaded to get down on its knees (as I recall it its knees seemed to bend the wrong way) and then Phillip climbedon to the wooden seat on its back with the little girl in front. When the camel rose to its feet in an ungainly fashion my poor husband turned a peculiar shade of grey and obviously was not enjoying swaying precariously so high up in the air. The camel was also somewhat smelly and had rather overpowering bad breath, not a surprise looking at its rotten teeth. The youngster had a lovely time and was ready for another ride when they finally dismounted but Phillip looked so ill that we were taken straight home. I believe he decided to forgo dinner that night.

We were informed by Marie that the annual *fête du melons* was to be held in Lectoure the weekend the girls were with us. The four of us accompanied the Boivins to the festivities. The centre of the city was separated into three main areas. In one there were throngs of teenagers dancing to disco music. Nearby, long wooden tables and benches were laid out for dinner and on the other side of the square there were various groups of performers, both singers and musicians. A line of men dressed much like Morris dancers in the U.K. walked past on huge stilts, leaning against lamp-posts when they stopped for a break. The meal featured melons in abundance as Gers is famous for its melons, half a melon (into which most of the diners poured red wine before eating it) for starters and melon again for dessert in addition to slices of apricot tart. In between we had salad with tuna and hard-boiled eggs and fried chicken. After dinner the tables were stacked away and the dancing began in earnest with whole families dancing together. When the golden oldies were played Phillip and I ventured onto the dance floor (the paved square) and enjoyed ourselves, much to the embarrassment of our young guests who probably thought we were too old for such frivolity. Our old friend the octogenarian was in fine form dancing the night away in spite of the vast quantities of red wine he had consumed during the meal.

One afternoon the girls disappeared. They hadn't told us they were going out so we looked everywhere on the property after a couple of hours, knowing they would not have gone on such a long walk in the heat. Eventually we found them fast asleep on top of the bales of hay in the open barn. They had climbed up with their books to read in the cool shade and had fallen asleep.

That winter we had new windows and a solid front door put in by Yves. The old door did not quite reach the doorsill so the hall was flooded every time there was a heavy downpour. We had had makeshift repairs done to the door before (by an Englishman living somewhere in Gascony who was looking for gardening and other odd jobs). His contribution consisted of a piece of plywood nailed to the bottom half of the door. It looked awful and did not keep the rain out. One of my first jobs on seeing this was to paint the bare plywood white as that was the only paint we had in Larroque – the door looked most peculiar with the bottom 18 inches white and the rest dark green! We decided we could do without any help in the garden apart from Pierre's occasional attack on the grass. The new door and shutters looked lovely and we spent hours applying the recommended undercoat and topcoat of wood stain. The only problem with doing up Larroque was that the renovated areas were so lovely that they showed up the rest of the problems. It was quite an expensive business as there was very little we could do ourselves because of lack of expertise and time.

The next summer we had a visitor from New Zealand. We had been well looked after by Liz when we stayed in her home during a lecture tour a couple of years before. I still drool over the memories of a fruit salad that she made with sliced tamarillos soaked in sugar overnight. When we returned to Guildford I was delighted to see tamarillos in Sainsbury's but they were disappointingly tasteless. Liz had planned to spend some time in Africa, then England before flying to Paris and on to Agen which was our nearest airport. The airport is very small and only small planes can land there but we were rather taken aback to see exactly how tiny the plane was. There were only three passengers and they were allowed just one small bag each – quite understandable on seeing the size of the plane. Liz had taken us sightseeing to many lovely areas in her country including a boat trip to see whales. Whilst we could not promise to do anything as exciting in Gascony we were pleased to take her to the *bastides* we knew and loved visiting. The Boivins insisted that the three of us have a meal with them and the cousins who were visiting at the time. As usual the meal was delicious though simple. We enjoyed having them (cousins included) for dinner at our place a few nights later and were pleased that they enjoyed my version of *cassoulet,* a regional dish made with beans, sausages, duck and/or lamb. I had decided to try out a recipe for pears braised in red wine as dessert. It tasted very good but the pears insisted on remaining pale instead of turning a rich red like the picture in the book.

Another summer our friends from Barcelona, Trini, José and their small baby son David, came to spend a weekend with us. We bought folding beds, and new bedlinen, pink, to match the curtains. The guest bedroom looked very pretty indeed with a bowl of fragrant pink roses from our garden. As Larroque is not easy to find, being somewhat off the beaten track, in addition to sending them a detailed map we tied balloons to the posts where our drive joined the main road. They were expected to arrive around 5pm as they had planned to leave home early in the morning. By 10pm we were becoming concerned and wondered whether we should go out looking for them. Eventually they arrived at 11pm, absolutely shattered, having had to stop several times because of the baby. However, they were used to late meals in Barcelona so were quite happy to have dinner at midnight once little David was fed, changed and put to bed. We were absolutely amazed at the variety of baby equipment they managed to fit into their car – a car seat, a small cot, a larger folding cot which would do until David was three, sterilising equipment, disposable nappies and the like. All these lovely transportable items were just not available when my children were little. I was a bit taken aback the next morning to see that all my lovely balloons had become deflated and were no longer landmarks.

We had a lovely weekend visiting our favourite *bastides*, enjoying ice cream while admiring the view along the river

Part of the buildings comprising the circular bastide we visited often.

from our seats on the pavement. Our guests had brought us some delicious ground coffee and a coffee percolator so we decided to buy the baby some presents from the baby store in our town. They had the most gorgeous little baby clothes (which must have been designed by a famous fashion house judging by the cost) which we could not resist buying along with a Beatrix Potter china bowl which reminded me of the one my children used, each passing it on to the next one in turn.

We still had no washing machine (or cooker) at Larroque so as soon as Trini and José departed I was washing sheets and towels by hand in preparation for our next visitor, Betty. My friendship with Betty goes back about 30 years, when we were at college together in St Albans. Betty was American, from Tennessee, I was from India and we got on like a house on fire. We have corresponded over the years and had met once about 15 years before when Betty, her husband Cliff and their children Bonnie and Greg visited us on their way back to the U.S. from Germany. Their children and ours were roughly the same age and indeed, had shared many of their baby clothes. I had persuaded Betty to visit us in France even if it meant coming on her own and was looking forward to catching up with all the news. Phillip and I met her at Agen railway station as she had flown to Paris and then changed to the TGV (the fast train, not Anna). Betty looked exactly the same as she did thirty years ago and we had a wonderful time reminiscing, occasionally remembering to fill in details for Phillip.

Betty, like Kay, is keen on gardening and could hardly wait to get into our untamed garden. Although I spent hours tidying it up and Phillip strimmed everything in sight each time we visited Larroque, it looked a mess when we arrived the next time and this visit was no exception. In a couple of days the undergrowth had been hacked away, the cannas saw the light of day

*The front of Larroque after renovation. The tree on the right now
has a little bird's nest in it.*

again and the brambles were attacked with vigour. I helped out
with clipping and pruning, shaping the bushes and shrubs yet
again. It was exciting to see a little bird's nest in our tree with
the red leaves. The birds had obviously accepted us. Again we
visited our favourite haunts, had coffee and ice cream at our
favourite café and dinner at the Pizzeria one night.

I had planned a trip to Provence as we had not been there
either and we set off early one morning, aiming to reach
Cavaillon by evening. We realised that the *autoroute* would be
the quickest way and only came off it to visit a beach on the
way. Another stop which was an absolute must was a visit to
Carcassonne, the Cathar fortress which is beautiful in all sea-
sons and at any time of day or night. There was a lot to see
including many little shops filled with tempting souvenirs. We
watched a procession enacting scenes from hundreds of years
earlier and felt sorry for the people in heavy armour. Lunch

and lots of cold drinks at a table under the shade of grapevines provided welcome relief from the scorching heat of the sun. We also had to have frequent stops for ice cream to cool off.

The hotel at Cavaillon had a walled-in courtyard which functioned as a garage. The only problem was that our hotel room overlooked the garage and proved to be extremely noisy with cars driving in and out all night, accompanied by loud conversations and laughter. Betty was more fortunate as her room was at the opposite end overlooking a small, quiet garden. After a bit of sightseeing the next day we drove to Ménerbes to see whether a statue of Peter Mayle had been erected in his honour! It hadn't! Roussillon was a must on our sightseeing trip as I had seen so many pictures of its beautiful rust-coloured soil and houses. There were coachloads of tourists and it proved impossible to get some lunch until they had all left. It was delicious when we finally were able to eat. Driving back through the hills of Provence we passed spectacular patchwork fields of pale and dark purple – the lavender fields in the valleys below. What was even more interesting was the way hundreds of tiny lavender plants were growing in crevices between the stones on the side of the hill, hundreds of feet above the valleys where the lavender fields were.

We introduced Betty to the Boivins and to Janet and then took her to our village *fête* where she thoroughly enjoyed herself. Both she and we were sorry when she had to leave. Back at Agen railway station it was interesting to note that her railway ticket had a blue stripe indicating where on the platform she should stand so that she would enter the right carriage – very civilised indeed.

We had noticed a row of beehives along the edge of our field that bordered our drive and thought they belonged to Pierre. One day we returned from shopping to see a little French van parked on this field and wondered whose it was. A little old French couple emerged and asked whether they could have their lunch in our field. It turned out that they owned the beehives and deposited them at various locations each summer, depending on which farmer was growing sunflowers. This year Pierre was using our field as well as his for sunflowers and ours was nearer the main road so the beehives were on our land. We invited them to have an *apéritif* with us (*pastis*, of course) before lunch and heard their story. The old man had been a farmer, his son now looked after the farm but he preferred to continue working for a living so decided to keep bees and sell the honey. He and his wife drove around the countryside collecting the honey each week in summer and paid the farmers with jars of honey. They then stayed at home by the fire during the winter months. We watched surreptitiously as they took a small folding table and chairs out of their van, placed them near our barn, laid a snowy white tablecloth and proceeded to enjoy their picnic lunch. It was such a pleasure seeing these two old folk, who must have been in their seventies, still enjoying a fruitful life together.

Chapter Twelve

A new beginning

During a visit to Larroque in 1997 we realised that all the space in the attic was being wasted and decided to do something about it. It extended over the length and breadth of the house and had lots of old beams and fairly solid floors. Of course, it was filthy, covered with owl droppings, cobwebs and tons of dust. The walls were exposed stone and more light was needed in the form of windows. The rickety staircase looked out of place in the renovated inner hall and climbing it was an occupational hazard. Yves was consulted yet again and we arranged to have the floors repaired and sanded, the walls plastered and a new staircase put in. We had forgotten that there was no ceiling – the roof tiles were arranged on wooden planks criss-crossing the beams. Yves mentioned that insulation and a new ceiling should be considered before starting on the walls. I also wanted a door in the wall facing south, opening onto a small balcony where we could look out at the peaceful view in summer, and another window to let in more light.

Estimates were given (expensive as always, but the workmanship was invariably superb!) and the work was to be completed by October. In my mind I had visualised the south facing room directly over the dining room as our bedroom, the area above the front bedroom would be our music room, behind it (over the guest bedroom) our library and the smaller area facing the back of the house (over the bread oven room) a dressing room.

We faxed Yves a few days before we were due to arrive asking whether the work had been completed and whether the house would be habitable. On hearing it would be ready we booked a flight to Toulouse as we intended to stay only two days and did not want to waste them driving from the ferry port to Larroque. We picked up a hired car at Toulouse airport that chilly November day and drove to our home. When we parked in front of the house we saw the front door wide open and heard loud music. There were piles of rubble everywhere just as once before, rotting planks, broken tiles and large stones in heaps at the side. No one seemed to be around when we went in but we could hear hammering upstairs. There was dust everywhere and the house was freezing. We walked around to the side and saw a huge gaping hole in the wall where the new door and balcony were to be put in. There was no way we could spend the night in Larroque without inhaling a ton of dust and freezing to death. We quietly got back into the car and drove straight back to Toulouse, fortunately managing to get a flight back to London that evening. Delays in getting work completed had become routine but we were not pleased at having wasted air tickets and a whole day with nothing accomplished. However, when the work was finally finished we returned to France and were thrilled with the results. The attic was bright and looked really lovely. All the beams had had to be injected for woodworm, the walls were a sparkling white as was the ceiling and the old wooden floor had been polished to a dull gleam. A brand new staircase had been installed which took some getting used to – each stair had only a half-step, alternately on the left and right. We now see the logic of half-steps in a short staircase. The wooden balcony was small but large enough for both of us to stand in side by side and lo and behold – we could see the Pyrenees very clearly in the winter light just as Henri had promised all those years ago.

We were invited to Yves' home for lunch to celebrate the near completion of Larroque – at least as much as we could afford to renovate for the time being. We jokingly told Yves he was probably a millionaire by now, what with the Larroque renovations and all the swimming pools he had installed over the years for other people. His house and garden were beautiful as one would expect from a builder and landscape gardener who loved his work. In the hall were two beautiful pieces of antique furniture – an *armoire* and a bureau. There were healthy plants all over the house making it look as though it was part of the garden. The solid wood cabinets in the kitchen had been constructed by Yves. There was a brick barbecue in the large terraced area and beyond that the swimming pool. At the far end of the garden was a lovingly restored ancient barn with walls of timber with a mixture of straw and clay packed in between. The fireplace in the dining room had been converted into a large spit on which was roasting a leg of venison – Yves had gone out hunting a few days before. He tended the roast venison while his lovely wife served the first courses. Inevitably we ate too much but had a thoroughly enjoyable afternoon.

In November 1997, totally unexpectedly, Phillip was asked to attend an interview for a job at Harvard Medical School. We enjoyed our trip to Boston although Phillip was obviously under a lot of stress and I was panicking, having being asked to give a lecture while we were there. All went well and Phillip was offered the job.

We were back in Boston in March 1998, this time for my job interviews and to look for a house as the move across the Atlantic was planned for June. We were both sorry to give up the jobs we had held for many years and to leave behind three of the children although they were now young adults living away from home. Kathryn and Andrea were still at University and Steve was working in the music business. Fortunately Sharon, who had been studying in the States for three years, first in Florida and now in New York, would be close to us and would be able to make up for all the time she had been away from home. The one thing Phillip and I both agreed on immediately was that we would sell our house in Guildford, although we were sorry to leave our kind neighbours, and keep Larroque as our base in Europe. We did consider the possibility of buying a small flat in London or Guildford but three mortgages would be disastrous even if our bank manager agreed in a moment of weakness.

House hunting in Boston was a unique experience. We had just two and a half days in which to find and buy a house. Preliminary telephone calls had enabled us to contact a Realtor (estate agent), Bob, who met us at our hotel with his colleague, Kim. We took to them instantly. They were extremely kind and went out of their way to be helpful. Not knowing anything about Boston we started looking at apartments (condominiums) in the city but found them quite expensive. Besides, we were planning to bring Snowy and Shandy with us and we therefore needed a yard (garden). It was like learning a new language after a manner of speaking. Two and a half bathrooms sounded strange until we discovered the half one was a W.C. We were a bit horrified at discovering that all the houses were built of wood apart from the chimney which was made of bricks. We immediately decided that we would never have a log fire no matter how cold it got in winter! Bob and Kim took us to see a few condos (condominiums) and then drove us west of the city to a beautiful part of Massachusetts where there were lovely woods and lakes with very attractive houses. We both knew at once when we saw our new house that it was the one for us and visited just one more as a reserve home in case things went wrong with the first one. We must have subconsciously had Larroque in our minds when we decided on the house we wanted – it was in a very quiet area at the end of a dead end road, the house backed onto a wooded hill and we owned part of the wood. A few minutes' walk through the woods at the side of the house led us to a lovely lake with a family of ducks floating serenely among waterlilies.

The next day Bob and Kim very kindly drove us to the bus station and, while waiting for Sharon, we signed the papers that Bob had brought. Fortunately all went well and we flew home after a short weekend with Sharon, hoping that all would go well with the sale. In the meantime we had to put our house in Guildford on the market in the hope it would sell immediately to pay the deposit on the American house. We also had to arrange for our old furniture to be shipped to Larroque, the best furniture, all our clothes and our work effects to be shipped to Boston, with enough clothes to manage for a few weeks in a hospital flat while we waited for our visas. The removal firm told us it would take them three days to pack all our earthly goods and we did our best to label as much as we could as soon as we had a completion date for the house sale. Inevitably a few items did go to the wrong country – my laptop, which should have stayed with me, was either in France or in a container somewhere on the high seas as were my certificates. I could not find my certificates or our marriage licence which was essential for me to obtain a visa so that I could accompany Phillip to Boston. It was amazing to find that three burly young men who would not have looked out of place on a soccer field, packed all of our household goods, including fine china and ornaments, with such care that not a single delicate item was broken on arrival. The night before the cleaning firm was to come in and tidy up in preparation for the new owners, Phillip and I were driving around Guildford trying to find a rubbish dump that was open at 2am. We had no idea how much rubbish we had accumulated over the past 12 years. Although the past few weekends had been spent filling a skip with unwanted belongings, both our cars were crammed with boxes of rubbish and old toys. It was not until the next day that we were able to get rid of the stuff.

The next few weeks were unsettling. We felt a bit like vagrants having sold our home and our cars, living out of suitcases and having to hire a car to go to France for a week's holiday before the flight to Boston.

We felt better once we were in Larroque – at least we had a home to return to if things went frightfully wrong in Boston. The house glowed golden yellow in the bright sunlight and the roses were in full bloom. The little trees in front of the house looked healthy and strong. The fresh countryside fragrance of flowers mingled with the mint we trampled underfoot started the unwinding process. With the attic completed there was very little dust indoors. Our friendly Alsatian from next door came over to greet us and we could hear the lowing of Janet's cows in the distance. We were home.

The furniture arrived the next day – boxes and boxes of neatly labelled possessions which rapidly filled the dining room and the bread oven room. On unpacking we discovered that we now had three dining tables, fourteen dining chairs, four wardrobes, four bedside cabinets, two double beds, three single beds and two folding beds at Larroque, not to mention the inflatable mattress of days gone by. There were three electric irons, two toasters and hundreds of books. There was so much china and glassware that we had to leave much of it in boxes as the cabinets were all overflowing. A new cupboard or sideboard will have to be gently mentioned to Phillip in the near future. Larroque now has enough furniture so that the whole family can visit and stay in comfort. Our old cooker, microwave oven and washing machine arrived intact and Yves has promised to do the wiring and plumbing before our next visit. The chimneys are also going to be blocked off in the hope that the field mice (there were a dozen little corpses this time) will then be unable to gain entrance to the house and access to our possessions. What a treat it will be to have a proper cooker at last in France although the Aga dream has not been abandoned as yet. I am determined to introduce the Boivins to scones and Yorkshire pudding, though not at the same time. The bedroom furniture was too big to be hauled up the narrow staircase into our beautifully renovated attic but Yves assured us it was not a problem. He would remove the railings from the balcony and lift the furniture into place through the door when we return to Larroque for our next holiday. How the furniture will actually be hauled up to the level of the balcony we are not sure but we are leaving it in Yves' capable hands.

Boston is a lovely city and adjusting to our new way of life has been painless. We arrived on a hot Saturday afternoon, accompanied by a vast amount of luggage and two crates, specially made, for Shandy and Snowy. The temperature in the cargo hold was raised so that they would be comfortable. They drew many admiring glances and comments from the airport staff and passengers at both Heathrow and Boston and seemed to have tolerated the seven-hour flight remarkably well. Shandy was obviously anxious to be let out of his box but the kennels had forgotten to put his lead in when they delivered him to the airport. We were thrilled to see Bob and Kim at the airport to meet us, going far beyond the call of duty. Kim asked a passing cleaner whether we could use a spare cord he had on his trolley and we now had a makeshift lead, to Shandy's delight. Bob, in the meantime accompanied Phillip to the car rental booth. We were so grateful Bob and Kim were there as we needed both cars to fit in all the baggage and the crates. We have made many other new friends and we cannot wait to have them come and stay with us at Larroque to enjoy the beauty of *La Belle France*.

Now that the children are a bit older they do want to visit Larroque even through there are no nightclubs near by. Sharon particularly wants to go horseriding as that is one of her favourite sports. On a recent visit to Boston Sharon and Phillip went riding with a group of people along Bobby's Trail. Being somewhat of a coward around large animals I stayed in the car and read. However, they looked as though they had had a good time when they returned and Phillip had no injuries at all so I decided to accompany them on their next ride. That was one of the biggest mistakes I have ever made. My horse, supposedly a docile one, first refused to budge, then trotted along half-heartedly so that the others were all out of sight including the little children in the group. The most embarrassing bit was that one of the helpers who obviously was a very good rider, had to wait for me because my horse was not cooperating. She suggested we change horses as mine knew her and would obey her orders. We did and my second horse then started to slow down. Just when I was wondering why it did not respond to my instructions it started cantering with me holding on grimly, bouncing up and down uncomfortably. To my relief this lady and I had to cut short our ride to catch up with the others who were trotting back to the ranch. I alighted stiffly vowing never to expose myself to the whims of a horse again. Sharon and Phillip can go riding in France, I shall find a less painful way to pass the time

Things have changed somewhat for the Boivins as well.

Dominique has moved into her home with Claude in a village a few kilometres away and they manage a *charcuterie*. Dominique makes all the *saucissons* and *saucisses* while Claude preserves *foie gras*. They are an industrious couple who should do well.

Marie and Pierre seem a bit lonely as François works elsewhere during the week but the whole family gathers together on Sundays to enjoy their *repas avec le 'ping'*.

Although we will not now be able to nip over to Larroque for the weekend whenever the fancy takes us, we are looking forward to the next visit when it will be a proper second home with all our English and French furniture and ornaments collected over the years. Perhaps it is now time to draw up plans for the stable conversion.

Léonie Press specialises in books about France,
particularly those detailing the lives and experiences of
non-French people who have moved to that country
or bought second homes there. These include:

A BULL BY THE BACK DOOR

How an English family find their own paradise in rural France
ANNE LOADER
Illus PATRICIA KELSALL
ISBN 1 901253 06 6, 192pp, paperback, £8.99,
146mm x 208mm, published 1997

THE DUCK WITH A DIRTY LAUGH

More family adventures in rural France
ANNE LOADER
Illus PATRICIA KELSALL
ISBN 1 901253 09 0, 218pp, paperback, £8.99,
146mm x 208mm, published 1998

ONLY FOOLS DRINK WATER

Forty years of fun in Charente-Maritime
GEOFFREY MORRIS
Illus PATRICIA KELSALL
ISBN 1 90125310 4, 106pp, paperback, £8.99,
146mm x 208mm, published 1999

If you would like to be added to our mailing list for
special offers on our books about France, please send us
a letter or drop us a line via e-mail. You can also keep
up-to-date by visiting our website.

Léonie Press, 13 Vale Road,
Hartford, Northwich,
Cheshire CW8 1PL
Tel: 01606 75660 Fax: 01606 77609
e-mail: anne@aloaderpubs.u-net.com (editorial)
jack@aloaderpubs.u-net.com (sales/marketing)
website: http://www.aloaderpubs.u-net.com